History and Functions of Government Departments

D1471918

London: H M S O

73 301
351 CEN Not to be taken away

Researched and written by Reference Services, Central Office of Information.

ISBN 0 11 701766 3

HMSO publications are available from:

HMSO Publications Centre
(Mail, fax and telephone orders only)
PO Box 276, London SW8 5DT
Telephone orders 071-873 9090
General enquiries 071-873 0011
(queuing system in operation for both numbers)
Fax orders 071-873 8200

HMSO Bookshops
49 High Holborn, London WC1V 6HB   071-873 0011
Fax 071-873 8200 (counter service only)
258 Broad Street, Birmingham B1 2HE   021-643 3740   Fax 021-643 6510
Southey House, 33 Wine Street, Bristol BS1 2BQ
0272 264306   Fax 0272 294515
9-21 Princess Street, Manchester M60 8AS   061-834 7201   Fax 061-833 0634
16 Arthur Street, Belfast BT1 4GD   0232 238451   Fax 0232 235401
71 Lothian Road, Edinburgh EH3 9AZ   031-228 4181   Fax 031-229 2734

HMSO's Accredited Agents
(see Yellow Pages)

and through good booksellers

Acknowledgments
The Central Office of Information would like to thank the government departments described in this book for their co-operation in compiling the text.

Cover Photograph Credit
Press Association

Contents

Introduction

As the chief means of giving effect to government policy, government departments play a vital role in the British[1] system of government. This book, as part of the Aspects of Britain series, describes the role they play in the context of the historical development of British public administration. Departments are grouped by different policy areas. Each section describes the history and development of a department, gives some examples of its policies and achievements, and sets out its current responsibilities. Each section also describes the executive agencies, executive and advisory bodies and tribunals for which departmental ministers are responsible. Details are given of each department's principal offices. Although all major departments other than the Scottish Office, Welsh Office and Northern Ireland Office have their headquarters in London, many have other offices in London and throughout the country. Some smaller departments are based outside London.

Related information on different aspects of government is available in some of the other titles in the Aspects of Britain series, including *Parliament* and *The British System of Government*. Forthcoming publications in the series will cover the civil service and executive agencies, and local government.

---

[1]The term 'Britain' is used informally in this book to mean the United Kingdom of Great Britain and Northern Ireland. 'Great Britain' comprises England, Scotland and Wales.

The Role of Government Departments

Government departments are the main instruments for implementing government policy when Parliament has passed the necessary legislation, and for advising ministers. They may, and often do, work with and through local authorities, statutory boards and government-sponsored organisations operating under various degrees of government control. A change of government does not necessarily affect the number or general functions of government departments, although major changes in policy may be accompanied by organisational changes.

The work of some departments (for instance, the Ministry of Defence) covers Britain as a whole. Other departments (such as the Department of Employment) cover England, Wales and Scotland, but not Northern Ireland. Others, such as the Department of the Environment, are mainly concerned with affairs in England. Some departments, such as the Department of Trade and Industry, maintain a regional organisation, and some which have direct contact with the public throughout the country (for example, the Department of Employment) also have local offices.

Most departments are headed by a minister and most of the ministers responsible for the major departments are members of the Cabinet. Where policy issues seldom arise departments may be headed by a civil servant, and a minister with other duties is responsible to Parliament for their actions. For example the Chancellor of the Exchequer is head of the Treasury, which has a key role in devising economic and financial policies, and has some responsibility for non-ministerial departments such as the Inland Revenue and HM Customs and Excise.

Ministers

Most ministerial departments are headed by a Secretary of State who sits in the Cabinet. In some instances the Cabinet minister in charge of a department may not be called Secretary of State but instead has a special title. For example, the Lord Chancellor (formally the Lord High Chancellor of Great Britain) heads the Lord Chancellor's Department. In some ministerial departments a Minister of State, who is not of Cabinet rank, is the departmental head. At present the Overseas Development Administration is headed by a Minister of State, and between 1979 and 1981 the Department of Transport was headed by a Minister of State who was not formally a member of the Cabinet, although he attended Cabinet meetings on a regular basis.

Ministers of State are usually appointed to work under a Secretary of State and may be given responsibility for a specific area of the department's functions; they may be given titles which reflect their duties. In the House of Lords, Government Whips may act as government spokesmen and women if the department concerned is not represented in the House.

Junior ministers usually have the title of Parliamentary Under-Secretary of State; when a department is not headed by a Secretary of State junior ministers are called Parliamentary Secretaries. Junior ministers share in parliamentary debates, answer parliamentary questions and assist in departmental duties.

In certain departments they are given specific responsibilities directly under the departmental minister.

All Secretaries of State and most Ministers of State are assisted by Parliamentary Private Secretaries. They are Members of Parliament (MPs) who help their ministers with routine tasks and often serve as a useful link with backbench MPs; unlike ministers they do not receive ministerial salaries.

Non-departmental Ministers

Non-departmental ministers usually include the holders of several traditional offices such as Lord President of the Council, Lord Privy Seal, Paymaster General and Chancellor of the Duchy of Lancaster. Occasionally Ministers without Portfolio are also appointed. Such ministers have few or no departmental duties and are therefore able to perform any special duties a Prime Minister might give them. In the present government the Chancellor of the Duchy of Lancaster is responsible for the Office of Public Service and Science. In previous Conservative Cabinets some of these posts have been combined with the non-governmental post of Chairman of the Conservative Party. For example, from 1990 to 1992 the Conservative Party Chairman, Chris Patten, sat in the Cabinet as Chancellor of the Duchy of Lancaster.

History of British Public Administration

The origin of British central administration lies in the committees of the medieval King's Councils (see p. 19) which were directly accountable to the ruling monarch. By the eighteenth century some of these committees had become departments headed by a single minister, but most existed in the form of boards and committees. In the years following the restoration of Charles II in 1660, boards and committees were used to administer key functions such as revenue collection and the Navy. Boards were preferred by monarchs because they were directly answerable to the Crown and not to a minister responsible to Parliament.

The office of Secretary of State can be traced back to the appointment of the King's Secretary during the reign of Henry III (1216–72). During the reign of Henry VIII (1509–47) Thomas Cromwell, the King's Secretary, became in effect Chief Minister; the post was subsequently occupied by men of great distinction such as Cecil (Lord Burleigh) and Walsingham. For much of the seventeenth and eighteenth centuries there were two Secretaries. The Southern Secretary was usually responsible for matters concerning Ireland, the colonies and relations with the mainly Catholic countries of southern Europe. The Northern Secretary was concerned with relations with the mainly Protestant countries of northern Europe. During the eighteenth century Secretaries of State for Scottish Affairs and colonial affairs were appointed for briefer periods. In the late eighteenth century public administration was reformed when the Northern and Southern Departments were dissolved and their functions transferred to newly created Foreign and Home Offices (see pp. 98 and 77).

In the late eighteenth and early nineteenth centuries some boards acquired the characteristics of ministries because power and responsibility became concentrated in the hands of a minister responsible to Parliament. For example responsibility for the Board of Trade, which was re-established in 1786, became concentrated in the President who was accountable to Parliament. Similarly, the Poor Law Board effectively became a ministry in 1847 when a minister accountable to Parliament was appointed as its head.

By the middle of the nineteenth century the use of boards had fallen out of favour. In the early 1850s most of the boards established before 1845 were reorganised or dissolved. For example, the General Board of Health became a ministry in 1854. It was felt that public administration should be in the hands of politicians accountable to Parliament. At the same time it was decided to centralise the main departments in Whitehall in London.

In the twentieth century new boards were created to administer many of the state's new economic and social functions. For example, in 1911 the Liberal Government created four Boards of Commissioners to run the new system of public health insurance. Advocates of boards argued that they were more efficient than ministries and that it was unwise to give politicians more power by creating ministries. These views were challenged by Viscount Haldane's *Report on the Machinery of Government* (1918), which claimed that boards were less responsible to Parliament than ministries. In 1919 a number of boards were replaced by ministries, for example, the Ministry of Transport supplanted the Road Board (see p. 53).

Despite Haldane's criticisms the use of boards, or quasi-governmental bodies as they came to be known, did not decline but increased. This expansion in the use of quasi-governmental bodies did not mean that the use of government departments declined; they remained the main institutions through which government policy was devised and executed.

Ministerial Responsibility

Ministers have collective and individual responsibility. The convention of collective responsibility means that ministers must support government policy or resign. The minister is also individually responsible for the work of his or her department. He or she is answerable for all its acts and omissions and must bear the consequences of any policy or administrative failures. This responsibility of ministers for their departments is an important means of bringing government under public control because the knowledge that failures might be scrutinised by Parliament and the public discourages arbitrary or incompetent behaviour.

Non-departmental Public Bodies

These organisations are public bodies for which ministers have a degree of accountability; they can be divided into three types, as follows.

Executive Bodies

Executive non-departmental public bodies conduct executive, administrative, regulatory or commercial functions. They have a large measure of independence over the conduct of day-to-day matters but usually operate within a policy framework established by a minister. These bodies normally employ their own staff and have their own budget. Executive bodies include the Arts Council, the Commission for Racial Equality and the Sports Council.

Advisory Bodies

This group consists mainly of bodies established by ministers to give them and their departments advice. Generally, advisory bodies do not employ their own staff or spend money. Advisory bodies include the Health Advisory Service and the Race Relations Employment Advisory Group.

Tribunals

Tribunals have jurisdiction in a specialised field of law and decide the rights and obligations of private citizens, and of government departments and local authorities. They are usually serviced by staff from their sponsor department. Tribunals include the Employment Appeal Tribunal, the National Health Service Tribunal and the Lands Tribunal.[2]

Executive Agencies

Since the launch of the Next Steps Initiative in 1988 the Government has been committed, as far as possible, to setting up separate agencies to perform the executive functions of government. Although they remain part of the Civil Service these agencies enjoy more freedom over pay, financial and personnel issues. A Chief Executive is responsible for the day-to-day operations of each agency, within a policy and resources framework set by the responsible minister and the Treasury. A full list of the executive agencies sponsored by each department is provided in the sections on individual departments.[3]

European Community and Other International Organisations

Britain's membership of the European Community and other international bodies such as the United Nations has a considerable

---

[2]For further details on the work of tribunals, see *Britain's Legal Systems* (Aspects of Britain: HMSO, 1993).
[3]For further details, see the forthcoming Aspects of Britain book on the Civil Service and executive agencies.

impact on the work of most government departments; many work closely with organisations in other countries, particularly in the European Community.[4]

[4]For further details, see *Britain in the European Community* (Aspects of Britain: HMSO, 1992).

Central Departments

Prime Minister's Office

10 Downing Street, Whitehall, London SW1A 2AA.Tel: 071-270
3000.

History and Development

The origin of the Prime Minister's Office, often known as Number
Ten, lies in the personal advisers and support staff who have serviced Prime Ministers since the post came into being in the
eighteenth century. Arrangements were put on a formal basis in
1900. The post of Principal Private Secretary emerged in the early
1900s and its holder became the head of the Prime Minister's staff.

As Prime Minister, Lloyd George created a think tank or pol-
icy unit at Number Ten in 1916. It was nicknamed the 'Garden
Suburb' because of its location in the garden of the Prime
Minister's residence. It processed information for the Prime
Minister, commented on departmental proposals coming to the
Prime Minister or the Cabinet, scrutinised the implementation of
policy and helped with the resolution of departmental disputes.
However, this administrative innovation did not survive beyond
the end of 1918.

When Winston Churchill became Prime Minister in 1940 he
brought personal advisers into Number Ten under Professor
Lindemann (later Lord Cherwell—see p. 31). These advisers
formed the Statistical Office and specialised in charts and statistics.

This office was dissolved in 1945 but was re-established, under Lord Cherwell, in 1951; it was finally abolished two years later.

In 1964 Harold Wilson (Prime Minister 1964–70 and 1974–76) created a Political Office to handle his constituency and political correspondence. In 1974, on regaining office, Wilson established a policy unit at Number Ten and staffed it with special advisers who had the status of temporary civil servants for the duration of their appointment. The term 'Prime Minister's Office' has been used to describe the Number Ten staff since the mid-1970s. Prime Ministers still make use of special advisers; for example, Margaret Thatcher appointed Sir Alan Walters and Sir Anthony Parsons to such posts.

Policies and Achievements

The policy unit has been involved in many key governmental decisions—for example, it assisted with the drafting of the White Paper on pay policy in 1977 and helped to develop the Citizen's Charter, which was published in July 1991.

Current Responsibilities

The Prime Minister's Office is responsible for providing the Prime Minister with administrative support through the Private Office. It is headed by a Principal Private Secretary. A Political Office supports the Prime Minister in his or her role as a party politician and Member of Parliament and is staffed by people on temporary appointments from outside the Civil Service. The Press Office, which is staffed by civil servants, handles media enquiries and briefs journalists.

The policy unit studies policy papers, researches the background to policy decisions, and seeks to identify potential problems at an early stage. The unit can suggest approaches that have been overlooked, acts as a think tank for new ideas and identifies neglected but important issues. It also has a role in monitoring the implementation of policy proposals. In addition, the Prime Minister receives advice from individuals appointed as special advisers in the Prime Minister's Office.

Offices

The Prime Minister's Office has been based in 10 Downing Street, the Prime Minister's residence, since it was created in about 1900. Its offices are next to those of the Cabinet Office.

Cabinet Office

Horse Guards Road, London SW1P 3AL. Tel: 071–270 5988.
70 Whitehall, London SW1A 2AS. Tel: 071–270 1234.

The civil servant at the head of the Cabinet Office is the Secretary of the Cabinet, who is also the Head of the Home Civil Service. At present the Chancellor of the Duchy of Lancaster heads the Office of Public Service and Science, which is based in the Cabinet Office.

History and Development

The origin of the Cabinet Office lies in the Secretariat of the Committee of Imperial Defence. The Defence Committee of the Cabinet was created in 1895 and was reformed in 1902, becoming the Committee of Imperial Defence. In 1904 the Committee of Imperial Defence was provided with a small permanent secretariat which was given responsibility for recording the Committee's decisions and discussions, collecting and co-ordinating information, preparing documents and memoranda and ensuring continuity in the treatment of issues by the committee.

The War Council absorbed the responsibilities of the Committee of Imperial Defence in 1914 and the secretariat was retained to serve the new organisation. In 1916 the Cabinet and War Committee (the new name for the War Council) were merged to form the War Cabinet and the secretariat began to serve this new body. In 1919 the Committee for Imperial Defence was re-established and the War Cabinet Secretariat divided its attention between the Cabinet and the Committee. This arrangement lasted until 1939 when the Committee of Imperial Defence was absorbed into the War Cabinet and its secretariat became part of the War Cabinet Secretariat.

A Central Economic Information Service was established in 1939 and in 1941 it was divided into the Economic Section of the War Cabinet Secretariat and the Central Statistical Office. The Economic Section was transferred to the Treasury in 1953 while the Central Statistical Office was given executive agency status and transferred to the Treasury in 1989.

In 1964 Harold Wilson (Prime Minister 1964–70 and 1974–76) appointed a staff of economic advisers under Thomas Balogh and a team of scientific advisers under Sir Solly Zuckerman, the Chief Scientific Adviser. In 1968 the Cabinet Office was separated from Treasury supervision and given its own Vote (that is, voted its own allocation of funds by Parliament).

In 1970 Edward Heath (Prime Minister 1970–74) created a Central Policy Review Staff (CPRS) and based it in the Cabinet Office. The CPRS was given responsibility for providing material and producing analyses to enable ministers to make informed policy decisions; however, it did not become a permanent part of the government machine and was abolished in 1983. In 1979 Margaret Thatcher (Prime Minister 1979–90) created an Efficiency Unit.

In 1981 the Cabinet Office acquired responsibility for civil service recruitment, personnel and training functions. At the same time, the Cabinet Secretary became joint head and then head of the Home Civil Service. Further reorganisation in 1987 led to the creation of the Office of the Minister for the Civil Service (OMCS), which was headed by a junior Minister who was also the Minister for the Arts. He had day-to-day responsibility for the Civil Service, a role delegated to him by the Prime Minister, who is the Minister for the Civil Service.

In 1992, with the addition of many new responsibilities, the Office of Public Service and Science (OPSS) was created under the Chancellor of the Duchy of Lancaster. Like OMCS before it, OPSS remains part of the Cabinet Office.

Current Responsibilities
The Cabinet Office Secretariat assists the Prime Minister in preparing the Cabinet agenda, passes on Cabinet decisions to departments, scrutinises the implementation of decisions taken in Cabinet and keeps the Cabinet minutes. The Cabinet Office also prepares official histories through its Historical and Records Section.

Office of Public Service and Science
70 Whitehall, London SW1A 2AS. Tel: 071–270 1234.
Horse Guards Road, London SW1P 3AL. Tel: 071–270 5988.

From summer 1993 the Office of Science and Technology will be based in Albany House, 86 Petty France, London SW1H 9EE. Tel: 071–217 2000.

The Chancellor of the Duchy of Lancaster is in charge of the OPSS and is a member of the Cabinet. He is supported by a Parliamentary Secretary. The OPSS is responsible for:

—raising the standard of public services across the public sector through the Citizen's Charter;

—improving the effectiveness and efficiency of central government, including, through the establishment of executive agencies, the market-testing programme and the promotion of best practice for the coherent management of people and resources; and

—advice, through its Office of Science and Technology headed by the Government's Chief Scientific Adviser, on science and technology policy, expenditure and the allocation of resources to the Research Councils.

Work by the OPSS to improve efficiency and effectiveness includes advice on the application of information systems and technology through the Government Centre for Information Systems. The OPSS also promotes openness in government.

The OPSS is also responsible for policy on the duties and responsibilities of civil servants; the recruitment and development of fast-stream civil servants; and the maintenance of a central list of people who wish to be considered for public appointments.

The OPSS has four executive agencies: the Civil Service College, Recruitment and Assessment Services, the Occupational Health Service and the Chessington Computer Centre. In addition, the Chancellor of the Duchy of Lancaster and the Parliamentary Secretary have ministerial responsibility for Her Majesty's Stationery Office and the Central Office of Information.

Non-departmental Public Bodies

The Cabinet Office sponsors the following non-departmental public bodies: one executive body—The Chequers Trust; seven advisory bodies—the Advisory Board for the Research Councils, the Advisory Committee on Business Appointments, the Advisory Council on Science and Technology, the Citizen's Charter Panel of Advisers, the Civil Service Appeal Board, the Political Honours Scrutiny Committee and the Security Commission; and five research councils—the Agricultural and Food Research Council, the Economic and Social Research Council, the Medical Research Council, the Natural Environment Research Council and the Science and Engineering Research Council.

Parliamentary Counsel

36 Whitehall, London SW1A 2AY. Tel: 071–210 6629.

This non-ministerial department is headed by the First Parliamentary Counsel. The Parliamentary Counsel were established in their modern form when the first full-time post was created in 1869. This change was introduced at a time when the Government was becoming responsible for a regular legislative programme and a more professional approach to the drafting of bills was required. The department was originally part of the Treasury and was called the Parliamentary Counsel to the

Treasury. In 1968 it became part of the Civil Service Department and its status as an independent department followed in 1970.

Parliamentary Counsel draft all government bills (primary legislation) except those relating exclusively to Scotland; these are handled by the Lord Advocate's Department (see p. 72). They also provide departments with advice on all aspects of parliamentary procedure relating to bills and draft government amendments to bills and parliamentary motions associated with their passage through Parliament. Recruitment is restricted to barristers and solicitors who, on appointment, undertake to abandon private practice.

Lord Privy Seal's Office

68 Whitehall, London SW1A 2AJ. Tel: 071-270 0502.

The office of the Lord Privy Seal originated in the use of official seals in ancient times. In the eleventh century, during the reign of Cnut (1016–35), seals were used as the means of authenticating documents. At a time of mass illiteracy, the presence of the correct seal was the most reliable sign that a document was genuine.

Medieval monarchs had a Great Seal, which was kept by the Chancellor. From at least the reign of John (1199–1216) the King also possessed a private seal (Privy Seal) which was used when the Great Seal was unavailable or considered too cumbersome. In 1275 a Keeper of the Privy Seal was appointed and in 1311 the Keeper was made a Minister of State.

In the fifteenth century the Privy Seal was separated from the Royal Household and its use became associated with financial matters. The use of the Privy Seal was discontinued in 1884, but the office of Lord Privy Seal was retained. By this time the holder of the post no longer had any personal involvement in the use of the seal and possessed other ministerial duties.

The successive holders of the office in the twentieth century have traditionally played an important part in Government with the holder of the office usually having a place in Cabinet. The absence of formal functions vested in the office have allowed its holder to undertake a variety of jobs. For example, Anthony Eden (Lord Privy Seal 1934–35) dealt with League of Nations matters, while John Anderson (1938–39) was responsible for improving air-raid precautions.

Since 1945 the office of Lord Privy Seal has been held on ten occasions by the Leader of the House of Lords and on six occasions by the Leader of the House of Commons.

The present Lord Privy Seal, a member of the Cabinet formed in April 1992, is Leader of the House of Lords and is responsible to the Prime Minister for the arrangement of business in that chamber. He also has a responsibility to the House itself to advise it on procedural matters and other difficulties as they arise. In addition he chairs a number of domestic and economic Cabinet Committees.

Lord President's Office

68 Whitehall, London SW1A 2AT. Tel: 071-270 4040.

The first Lord President of the Council was appointed towards the end of Henry VII's reign (1485–1509). The Lord President chaired the Privy Council in the King's absence and acted, with the Chancellor, the Treasurer and the Lord Privy Seal, as an executive committee. In the sixteenth century the post was often vacant and it was not until the seventeenth century that it was permanently occupied.

The Lord President, who is a member of the Cabinet, presents the business to the Queen and her Counsellors at the formal meetings of the Privy Council. He is also responsible for the Privy Council Office (see below). Because few departmental duties exist, the Lord President is usually given special responsibilities. For example, Lord Woolton (Lord President 1951–52) co-ordinated agriculture and food policies, Lord Hailsham (1957–59 and 1960–64) combined the post with science and education and Richard Crossman (1966–68) had responsibility for co-ordinating health and social security policies. Lord Whitelaw (when Lord President 1983–88) and Sir Geoffrey Howe (1989–90) also served as Deputy Prime Minister and it has become customary for the Lord President to answer Prime Minister's Questions in the House of Commons when the Prime Minister is away.

In recent times the Lord President has also been Leader of the House of Commons. In this capacity the Lord President is responsible for supervising the Government's legislative programme in that chamber. The Lord President also upholds the rights and privileges of the House and moves procedural motions.

Privy Council Office

Whitehall, London SW1A 2AT. Tel: 071–270 3000.

William the Conqueror (1066–87) established the Great Council, which was composed of the country's leading men. The Council helped to decide state policies, supervised the work of the administration, sat as the highest court and occasionally made laws.

The Great Council usually met only three times a year and therefore had to devolve its powers to the *Curia Regis* (or Little Council) so that the King's government could continue when it was not sitting. As meetings of the Great Council became more infrequent the workload on the *Curia Regis* increased and it created a Permanent Council to handle its non-judicial work. By the reign of Henry VI (1422–61) the Permanent Council had itself become too large and a Privy Council was created from the former body.

In the eighteenth century much of the role of the Privy Council was assumed by the Cabinet, which became the effective forum within which government decisions were taken, although the Council retained certain executive functions. Some government departments originated as committees of the Privy Council. In 1833 the Judicial Committee was set up as a court of appeal from ecclesiastical and overseas courts.

The Privy Council's main function nowadays is to advise the monarch to approve Orders in Council and on the issue of royal proclamations. The council also has supervisory powers over the registering bodies for the medical and allied professions. The Judicial Committee of the Privy Council is the final court of appeal from courts of British dependencies, the Channel Islands, the Isle of Man, some Commonwealth countries and certain professional and disciplinary committees and church sources.

The Privy Council Office, which conducts administrative work for the Privy Council, is headed by the Lord President of the Council (see above). It is responsible for issuing Orders in Council, for handling applications for the grant or amendment of royal charters and associated by-laws, for formalities connected with ministerial changes, and for arranging the appointment of High Sheriffs.

Economic, Financial and Industrial Departments

HM Treasury

Parliament Street, London SW1P 3AG. Tel: 071–270 3000.

The office of Lord High Treasurer has been in commission since 1714 (meaning that responsibility passed from an individual minister to a board). The Lord High Commissioners of the Treasury consist of the First Lord of the Treasury (who is also the Prime Minister), the Chancellor of the Exchequer and five junior Lords, who serve as Government Whips in the House of Commons. In practice the Commissioners never meet as a board and the running of the department is conducted by the Chancellor of the Exchequer, who is a Cabinet minister.

The Chancellor is currently assisted by a Chief Secretary, who is also a member of the Cabinet, a Financial Secretary, an Economic Secretary and the Paymaster General. The Parliamentary Secretary to the Treasury is the Government Chief Whip.

History and Development

The Treasury originated in the treasuries that formed part of the households of Saxon and Norman monarchs. It was headed by the Lord High Treasurer, one of the great medieval offices of state.

In 1580 the Lord High Treasurer appointed a secretary with responsibility for receipts and expenditure on the Navy, the Crown's land forces and the Royal Household. In the seventeenth century James I (1603–25) and Charles I (1625–49) put the Treasury into commission at regular intervals and gave the duties of the Lord Treasurer to a board of five or six privy counsellors. As a result it became increasingly important to have regular procedures and a competent secretary.

In 1667 Charles II (1660–85) appointed a new type of commission which did not include any of the main privy counsellors apart from the Chancellor of the Exchequer. Under the new Secretary, Sir Charles Downing, the first real system of Treasury records was kept.

The practice of putting the Treasury into commission and the decision to make it independent of the Privy Council led to the First Lord of the Treasury becoming known as the Prime Minister in 1721. As a result of the wider responsibilities of the office of Prime Minister, the First Lord of the Treasury relinquished day-to-day control of the Treasury to the Chancellor of the Exchequer.

In the early eighteenth century the Treasury Board met frequently with the monarch in the chair. The monarch ceased to attend after George III (1760–1820) surrendered royal revenues in return for the Civil List.[5] In the nineteenth century meetings became less frequent; they were discontinued after 1856.

Taxation proceeds were paid into a number of separate funds, but in 1787 a Consolidated Fund was created and from that date government revenues, with a few exceptions, have been administered through this single fund.

[5]For further details, see *The Monarchy* (Aspects of Britain: HMSO, 1991).

Until 1866 there were no comprehensive audited accounts of government expenditure and the Treasury had virtually no knowledge of how other departments had spent their funds. It could not therefore exercise control over the way in which government moneys were spent. In 1866 this changed with the creation of the post of Comptroller and Auditor General. This officer, who was answerable to Parliament and therefore independent of the executive, was made responsible for auditing government expenditure. With the co-operation of the Comptroller and Auditor General and the House of Commons Public Accounts Committee, which had been established in 1861, the Treasury was able to hold the rest of the government machine to account for its use of public funds.

In 1870 open competition for entry into the Civil Service was established following the recommendations made in the Northcote/Trevelyan Report (see p. 24). The responsibility for the selection of candidates was vested in the Civil Service Commission and Treasury ministers were made answerable to Parliament for the Commission's activities. The Treasury also acquired responsibility for conditions of service in the Civil Service and for approving the entrance regulations set by the Commission.

After the first world war the Treasury expanded its role in staffing matters and acquired a new responsibility for negotiating with staff representatives. Following the publication of the Assheton Report in 1944 a higher priority was given to Civil Service training.

The Treasury acquired responsibility for economic co-ordination and planning in 1947, and in 1953 the Economic Section of the Cabinet Office was transferred to it. In 1962 the Treasury was re-organised into two divisions, one responsible for finance and economic matters and the other covering Civil Service pay and management.

Responsibility for long-term economic planning was transferred to the Department of Economic Affairs in 1964 but was regained after that department was abolished in 1969. Following the recommendations of the Fulton Report on the structure, recruitment and management of the Civil Service, the Treasury lost its responsibility for Civil Service pay and management to the new Civil Service Department in 1968. The Department was abolished in 1981 and functions relating to Civil Service pay, numbers, allowances and pensions were returned to the Treasury.

In 1992 the Treasury reformed its internal management structure and established a management board to replace the policy coordinating committee, which considered broad economic issues, and several other groups which considered internal management issues. The new board consists of the department's top ten officials and meets once a week.

Policies and Achievements

William Gladstone (Chancellor of the Exchequer 1852–55, 1859–66, 1873–74 and 1880–82) did much to reform the Treasury. Gladstone established the Northcote/Trevelyan Committee, implemented its proposal to create a Civil Service Commission, and devised the Exchequer and Audit Departments Act (1866) which created the post of Comptroller and Auditor General.

David Lloyd George (Chancellor of the Exchequer 1908–15) increased income tax, created a super tax, established a new land tax and raised death duties in order to pay for social reforms such as the introduction of old age pensions. James Callaghan (Chancellor of the Exchequer 1964–67) introduced capital gains tax and corporation tax and Anthony Barber (1970–74) established value added tax (VAT). Sir Geoffrey Howe (1979–83) abolished Exchange controls while Nigel Lawson (1983–89) reformed corporation tax.

Current Responsibilities

The Treasury is responsible for the formulation and implementation of economic policy, the central framework of Civil Service management and pay, the planning of taxation and spending, and the general oversight of the financial system. Its responsibilities extend throughout Britain. The Chief Secretary, the Economic Secretary, the Paymaster General and the Financial Secretary each have specific responsibilities. The present duties of these ministers are listed below.

The Chief Secretary's brief covers the planning and control of public spending, public sector pay, including nationalised industry pay and value for money in the public services (including the Next Steps programme—see p. 8).

The Financial Secretary is currently responsible for the voting of funds by Parliament, other parliamentary financial business such as the Public Accounts Committee, oversight of the Inland Revenue (excluding the Valuation Office) and Inland Revenue taxes (except stamp duties). The Financial Secretary also deals with privatisation, wider share-ownership policies, Civil Service pay and personnel management, and competition and deregulation policy.

The Paymaster General currently handles Customs and Excise duties, taxes and general oversight, European Community Budget and future financing, personnel management, the environment (including energy efficiency), charities (including pay-roll giving) and the Paymaster General's Office.

The Economic Secretary is currently responsible for monetary policy (including funding), the Department for National Savings, the Registry of Friendly Societies and the National Investment and Loans Office and Treasury responsibilities for the financial system. The Economic Secretary is also responsible for the Central Statistical Office and the Royal Mint (both executive agencies), the Government Actuary's Department, FORWARD Civil Service Catering, the Valuation Office, international financial issues and institutions (apart from the EC), Treasury Bulletin and Economic Briefing, North Sea oil and oil taxation.

Non-departmental Public Bodies

Advisory bodies sponsored by the Treasury include the Top Salaries Review Body and the Royal Mint Advisory Committee.

Offices

Treasury business was conducted at the Exchequer Receipt Office in Westminster Cloisters until Charles II (1660–85) put the Treasury into commission in 1660. The King moved the department to Whitehall Palace where it remained until the palace was destroyed by fire in 1698. For six weeks the Treasury was accommodated in the private house of William Lowndes, near Westminster Abbey. In February 1698 William III (1688–1702) gave the Treasury new chambers at Henry VIII's Cockpit on the west side of Whitehall. In 1733 work began on rebuilding the Treasury Office on the Cockpit site. The old Cockpit lodgings were demolished and a new Treasury building on the south side of Horse Guards Parade was constructed in 1753.

The present Treasury building was built on five acres of land enclosed by Parliament Street, King Charles Street, Great George Street and St James's Park. This area was cleared under the Public Offices, Westminster Site Act 1896 in order to build government offices. The section of the building fronting Parliament Street was started in 1900 and finished in 1907; by 1915 work had been completed on the second section facing Great George Street and St James's Park.

The building, which was designed by J.M. Brydon, is in the English Renaissance style. The exterior is faced with Portland stone and the entrance halls and staircases giving access to Storey's Gate, St James's Park, Parliament Street, Great George Street and King Charles Street are constructed in Mezzaro marble.

Although the building was originally constructed for the Board of Education and the Local Government Board, it has been occupied by a range of departments such as the Department of Economic Affairs and the Civil Service Department. The Treasury has occupied this building since the early 1940s. The address was given as Great George Street until 1972, when it was changed to Parliament Street.

HM Customs and Excise

New King's Beam House, 22 Upper Ground, London SE1 9PJ. Tel: 071–620 1313.

This non-ministerial department is headed by a Chairman with a Board of Commissioners. The Chancellor of the Exchequer has a degree of responsibility for its actions and one of the Treasury ministers is responsible for the department.

History

Duties on imported goods have been collected in England since the eighth century and *The Ancient and Rightful Customs* are mentioned in Magna Carta (1215). Customs Commissioners were appointed in 1671 to manage the service in England and Wales and a separate Board of Commissioners for Scotland was set up in 1707. Following the Union a single Board of Customs for Britain was established in 1823 and the separate administration of the Scottish and Irish customs ceased.

The first excise duties (taxes levied on goods produced or sold within the country, and on various licences) were levied by Parliament in 1643 in order to provide funds for its army during the English Civil War, and commissioners were appointed after the restoration of the monarchy in 1660. In 1849 the board was merged with the Board of Stamps and Taxes to form the Board of the Commissioners of the Inland Revenue (see p. 29). The administration of excise duties was transferred to the Customs Department in 1909; it was later renamed the Board of Customs and Excise. In 1947 its responsibility for the payment of non-contributory old age pensions to pensioners not receiving national assistance passed to the Assistance Board.

Current Responsibilities

The department is responsible for the administering and collecting of excise duties and VAT, and advises the Chancellor of the Exchequer on issues connected with them. Customs and Excise is also responsible for detecting and preventing evasion of revenue laws and enforcing restrictions and prohibitions on the importation of certain goods. The department undertakes agency work for other departments, including the compilation of overseas trade figures from export and import documents. Its responsibilities extend throughout Britain.

The department is relocating some of its headquarters work. Several directorates moved to Liverpool and Manchester during 1991 and this relocation programme will continue until 1995.

Board of the Inland Revenue

Somerset House, London WC2R 1LB. Tel: 071–438 6622.

The Board is headed by a Chairman. The Chancellor of the Exchequer is responsible to Parliament for the Inland Revenue. A Board of Taxes was created in 1784 to replace the bodies handling the assessed taxes, which were paid on luxury items. In 1833 the Board of Taxes was merged with the Board of Stamps (established in 1694) to form the Board of Stamps and Taxes. The Board of the Inland Revenue was formed in 1849 when the Board of Stamps and Taxes was amalgamated with the Board of Excise. Excise was the responsibility of the Inland Revenue until 1909 when it passed to the Board of Customs and Excise (see p. 28).

Unlike the notional boards that developed from the Privy Council in the eighteenth and nineteenth centuries, this board has a practical day-to-day purpose. It is composed entirely of civil servants called commissioners. The Board is responsible for Inland Revenue taxes and has the powers necessary for the performance of this duty. Ministers do not have to concern themselves with the detailed administration of tax law and the possibility of political interference in specific cases is therefore removed.

In the 1980s this department played a major part in pioneering the extension of information technology in the Civil Service when the Pay-As-You-Earn (PAYE) income tax system was computerised.

The Board of the Inland Revenue is responsible for the administration and collection of direct taxes throughout Britain. The main taxes within its remit are income tax, corporation tax, capital gains tax, petroleum revenue tax, inheritance tax and stamp duty. The Board also advises the Chancellor of the Exchequer on policy issues relevant to its responsibilities.

Most of the department's work in assessing and collecting tax and duty, together with the provision of many internal services, is now carried out by 34 executive offices, formed as part of the Next Steps programme.

The Board's Valuation Office is organised as an executive agency. This office is responsible in England, Scotland and Wales for the valuation of land and buildings for taxes administered by the Board. In Northern Ireland valuation services are the responsibility of the province's Department of Finance and Personnel (see p. 117). The Valuation Office assists and advises other departments by providing furnishing valuations and conducting negotiations concerned with the acquisition, issue and sale of land. It performs similar functions for local authorities and other public and local bodies.

The Valuation Office also prepares and maintains rating lists in England and Wales, provides the Government with a directing and valuation service for the council tax, and runs a land advisory service for other government departments.

Tribunals sponsored by the department include the General Commissioners of Income Tax.

Paymaster General's Office

Sutherland House, Russell Way, Crawley, West Sussex RH10 1UH. Tel: 0293 560999.

The formal head of this department is the Paymaster General, who is at present a Minister of State at the Treasury. In practice, the Assistant Paymaster General, who is a permanent official, is the department's head. The department became an executive agency in April 1993.

This office was created in 1835 by the amalgamation of the four pay offices: those of the Paymaster General of the Forces, the Paymaster and Treasurer of Chelsea Hospital, the Treasurer of the Navy and the Treasurer of Ordnance. In 1848 the offices of the Paymaster of the Civil Service and the Paymaster of the Exchequer Bills were also incorporated.

The Paymaster General's Office serves as the paying agent for government departments apart from the revenue departments and is responsible for the payment of 1.5 million public service pensions.

The Paymaster General's powers are delegated to the permanent staff of the Paymaster General's Office. The present incumbent, Sir John Cope (Paymaster General since 1992), is a Minister of State at the Treasury and is responsible for a number of Treasury matters (see p. 25).

Former Paymasters General have been responsible for a wide range of issues. Lord Cherwell (Paymaster General 1942–45 and 1951–53) was responsible for the Prime Minister's Statistical Office (see p. 10). Lord Belstead (Paymaster General 1990–92) was a Minister of State at the Northern Ireland Office.

Ministry of Agriculture, Fisheries and Food

Whitehall Place, London SW1A 2HH. Tel: 071–270 3000.

The Ministry is headed by the Minister of Agriculture, Fisheries and Food, who is a Cabinet minister and is currently assisted by a Minister of State and two Parliamentary Secretaries of State.

History and Development

The Board of Agriculture, which was created in 1889, was charged with promoting the general welfare of agriculture and publishing agricultural information and statistics. The Board also acquired the functions of a Privy Council Committee relating to animal diseases and was given the responsibilities of the Land Commission relating to allotments, tithe commutation, land drainage and improvements, copyhold (an old form of land tenure) and enclosures.

In 1903 the Board of Agriculture and Fisheries was created by the merger of the Board of Agriculture and the Fisheries Department of the Board of Trade, which had been established in 1886. The Board became a ministry in 1919 and was given responsibility for agriculture and fisheries in England and Wales but not in Scotland or Ireland. The Ministry of Food was first established in 1916 to deal with food shortages arising from the first world war and was abolished in 1921, its remaining functions being allocated mainly to the Board of Trade. It covered all four countries. In 1939 the Ministry of Food was re-established to handle food problems arising from the second world war.

In 1951 the work of the Ministry of Agriculture and Fisheries and the Ministry of Food was placed under the supervision of the Lord President of the Council who was able to co-ordinate the activities of both ministries. This 'overlordship' system ended in 1953, but the ministries were merged in 1955 to form the Ministry of Agriculture, Fisheries and Food. In 1968 the Welsh Office was given responsibility over a range of agriculture and fisheries issues affecting the Principality. Ten years later full responsibility for agriculture and fisheries in Wales passed to the Welsh Office although the Ministry of Agriculture, Fisheries and Food retained responsibility for food throughout Britain.

Policies and Achievements

In the 1930s the Ministry of Agriculture established several marketing boards, such as the Milk Marketing Board, to promote particular agricultural industries. In 1947 Thomas Williams (Minister for Agriculture and Fisheries 1945–51) introduced the first of a series of Agriculture Acts which created a system of government support based on an annual price review. Government subsidies maintained price levels and farmers received a guaranteed price regardless of how much they produced.

The system of agricultural support was changed after Britain joined the European Community in 1973. Under the European Community's Common Agricultural Policy the farmer obtains a guaranteed price through the imposition of tariff barriers against non-European Community food; surpluses are bought by the Community and stored. The system is, however, expensive and since 1980 various reform plans have been proposed and implemented. British Ministers of Agriculture, Fisheries and Food have been in the forefront of the reform.

Current Responsibilities

The Ministry is responsible for government policies on fisheries, agriculture and horticulture in England and for food safety and quality in Britain as a whole.[6] The negotiation and administration of European Community common agricultural and fisheries policies are also the responsibility of the ministry along with relevant issues arising from the single European market. This department is also responsible for international food trade and agricultural policy.

The Ministry gives grants to help farmers maintain efficient farming systems, while also meeting the cost of combating pollution and conserving the countryside. It is also responsible for policies for the control and eradication of animal, plant and fish diseases. It has responsibilities relating to the enhancement and protection of the countryside and marine environment, flood defence, appropriate research and development, and a range of other rural issues.

Responsibility for public health standards in the manufacture, preparation and distribution of basic foods falls within the Ministry's remit, which also covers the planning and safeguarding of essential food supplies in emergencies. Government relations with the British food and drink manufacturing industries and the food and drink importing, distributing and catering trades are also handled by the Ministry.

The Food Safety Directorate has responsibility for many aspects of food quality and safety. These include pesticide registration and safety approval, animal health and welfare, analytical and research work, biotechnology and meat hygiene.

---

[6]For further information on current policies, see *Agriculture, Fisheries and Forestry* (Aspects of Britain: HMSO, 1993).

The Ministry is responsible for six executive agencies: the Agriculture Development and Advisory Service, the Central Science Laboratory, the Central Veterinary Laboratory, the Intervention Board Executive Agency, the Veterinary Medicines Directorate and the Pesticides Safety Directorate.

Non-departmental Public Bodies
Executive bodies sponsored by the Ministry include the Sea Fish Industry Authority, the Meat and Livestock Commission and the Apple and Pear Research Council. Advisory bodies include the Food Advisory Committee and the Farm Animal Welfare Council. There are four tribunals: the Agricultural Land Tribunals, the Dairy Produce Quota Tribunal, the Milk and Dairies Tribunals (England) and the Plant Varieties and Seeds Tribunal. The Ministry also sponsors one public corporation: the Covent Garden Market Authority.

Offices
Following its creation in 1955 the Ministry was housed at 3 Whitehall Place, the old home of the Ministry of Agriculture and Fisheries, 10 Whitehall Place, and Dean Bradley House in Horseferry Road which had been the base of the Ministry of Food. Since 1956 the Ministry's headquarters has been at the Whitehall Place site.

Department of Employment

Caxton House, Tothill Street, London SW1H 9NF. Tel: 071–273 3000.

The Department is headed by a Secretary of State, who is a member of the Cabinet. At present there are also one Minister of State and two Parliamentary Under-Secretaries of State.

History and Development

The Ministry of Labour was created in 1916 and in the following year took over the Labour Exchange Service, including the administration of unemployment benefit, wages councils and industrial relations work from the Board of Trade. With the fall of the Coalition Government in 1922 responsibility for employment issues was concentrated in this ministry. It collected most of the employment statistics, ran the employment placing service, administered unemployment insurance, handled most industrial relations matters and administered the Trade Boards Acts.

In 1939 the department was renamed the Ministry of Labour and National Service with added responsibility for mobilisation of labour for industry and conscription in the armed forces. In 1940 responsibility for the Factory Acts was transferred from the Home Office, but in 1945 responsibility for unemployment insurance was passed to the Ministry of National Insurance. With the abolition of national service in 1959 the title reverted to the Ministry of Labour.

In 1968 the Ministry took over responsibility for supervising the prices and incomes policy from the Department of Economic Affairs and was renamed the Department of Employment and Productivity. The Conservative Government removed the department's responsibility for monopolies, mergers and restrictive trade practices in 1970 and gave them to the new Department of Trade and Industry. At the same time the Department's name was changed to the Department of Employment.

In 1973 and 1974 the Department lost many of its executive functions which were given to what later became known as executive non-departmental public bodies. Job-finding and training services were transferred to the Manpower Services Commission; responsibility for health and safety matters passed to the Health and Safety Executive; and the Department's industrial conciliation and arbitration services were transferred to the Advisory, Conciliation and Arbitration Service (ACAS).

Between 1985 and 1987 the Department was responsible for inner city matters. Responsibility for tourism was obtained from the Department of Trade and Industry in 1986 but passed to the Department of National Heritage in 1992. Responsibility for small firms was obtained from the Department of Trade and Industry in 1986 but was passed back in 1992. In 1987 the Jobcentre network was taken from the Manpower Services Commission and merged with the Department's unemployment benefit service to form the Employment Service, which became an executive agency in 1990. In 1988 the Training Commission was itself abolished and its functions were transferred to an executive agency based in the department. Responsibility for the co-ordination of government policy on issues of particular interest to women was added in 1992.

Although the statutory name remains the Department of Employment, the familiar name was changed in 1988 to the Employment Department.

Policies and Achievements
Since the late 1960s the Department has introduced much legislation concerning the trade unions and industrial relations. Barbara Castle (Secretary of State for Employment and Productivity 1968–70) introduced an Industrial Relations Bill based on the

White Paper *In Place of Strife* but failed to see it enacted. Robert Carr (Secretary of State for Employment 1970–72) introduced an Industrial Relations Court, but this proved to be short-lived.

James Prior (1979–81) restricted lawful picketing and limited the closed shop, while Norman Tebbit (1981–83) increased compensation for those dismissed due to the closed shop and reduced the legal immunities enjoyed by trade unions. Tom King (1983–85) introduced regular elections for trade union officials and Norman Fowler (1987–90) increased the rights of individual trade unionists to ignore a strike call and abolished the national dock labour scheme.

In 1970 Barbara Castle introduced the Equal Pay Act, and Michael Foot (1974–76) established new conditions, through the Employment Protection Act 1975, altering ways in which employers could dismiss their employees.

Current Responsibilities

The Department of Employment is responsible for the promotion of an efficient and competitive labour market conducive to the reduction of unemployment and the growth of employment. Its main duties are to help people obtain and improve their skills and competence for work, to encourage industry to train its workforce, to promote the creation and growth of self-employment and small firms, and to assist the unemployed.

Equal opportunities policy, the co-ordination of government policy relating to women, statistics on labour and industrial matters, employment policy and legislation and the careers service fall within the Department's brief. The Secretary of State is also responsible for establishing the strategic policy framework in consultation with the Secretaries of State for Scotland and Wales.

Many of the Department's executive functions are conducted through non-departmental public bodies and other public organisations which report to the Secretary of State (see below).

The Employment Service is charged with assisting people to find jobs and thereby helping employers to fill their vacancies. The Service also administers the payment of unemployment benefit and it is creating a network of integrated job centres to establish a single point of access to government training and employment programmes and services for the unemployed.

A network of independent Training and Enterprise Councils in England and Wales and Local Enterprise Companies in Scotland is responsible for planning and delivering government-funded training and enterprise programmes.

The Department's responsibilities cover England, Scotland and Wales apart from its responsibility for the careers service, which is limited to England. It represents the whole of Britain in international employment discussions.

Non-departmental Public Bodies

Executive bodies sponsored by the Department include the Advisory, Conciliation and Arbitration Service and the Health and Safety Executive. Advisory bodies include the Race Relations Employment Advisory Group and the Advisory Committee on Women's Employment. There are four tribunals: the Central Arbitration Committee, the Employment Appeal Tribunal, the Industrial Tribunals and the Levy Exemption Referees.

Offices

The Department's London headquarters are in Caxton House, Tothill Street. From 1941 to 1979 the Department of Employment and its predecessor departments were based in St James's Square. The first home of the Department from 1917 to 1941 was in Montagu House, Whitehall.

Department of the Environment

2 Marsham Street, London SW1P 3EB. Tel: 071–276 0900.

The current ministerial team is composed of a Secretary of State, who sits in the Cabinet, a Minister of State for Housing and Planning, a Minister of State for Local Government and Inner Cities, a Minister of State for the Environment and Countryside and three Parliamentary Under-Secretaries of State.

History and Development

In 1919 the creation of the Ministry of Health brought health, housing and local government functions within a single department. Planning functions were transferred to the Ministry of Works in 1942 and given their own ministry the following year when the Government created a Ministry of Town and Country Planning.

In its 1945 general election manifesto the Labour Party pledged to create a Ministry of Housing and Planning, combining the housing powers of the Ministry of Health and the planning powers of the Ministry of Town and Country Planning. In 1950 a government inquiry observed that the Ministry of Town and Country Planning was too small and recommended that its functions be returned to the Ministry of Health.

A modified form of the inquiry's recommendations was implemented in 1951 when the local government responsibilities of the Ministry of Health were combined with those of the Ministry of Town and Country Planning to form the Ministry of Housing and Local Government. In 1966 the responsibilities of the Ministry of Land and Natural Resources were added, following the abolition of that ministry. The Ministry of Housing and Local Government therefore acquired responsibility for a range of issues such as allotments, common land, forestry policy, the National Parks, leasehold enfranchisement, the Ordnance Survey, tree preservation, water, rent apportionments and the establishment of a Land Commission. The Ministry was also charged with ensuring the availability of land and natural resources for the community.

A ministerial 'overlord', Anthony Crosland, was appointed in 1969 to cover the Ministries of Transport and Housing and Local Government in order to integrate the Government's approach to housing, planning and transport. In 1970 the new Government took this strategy a stage further and amalgamated the two ministries to form the Department of the Environment. This new department also acquired the functions of the Ministry of Public Building and Works which had been responsible for the construction industry, government buildings, royal palaces, royal parks, the preservation of ancient monuments and historic buildings and the Government's buildings programme. The Department also obtained responsibility for sport from the Department of Education and Science.

The Ministry of Transport was re-established in 1976 and responsibility for sport returned to the Department of Education and Science in 1990. In 1992 responsibility for royal palaces, royal parks, and the preservation of historic buildings and ancient monuments passed to the Department of National Heritage. The

Department of the Environment gained responsibility for inner city task forces and energy efficiency.

Policies and Achievements

On several occasions the Department has been responsible for the reorganisation of local government boundaries. Under the first Secretary of State, Peter Walker (1970–72), some ancient counties such as Rutland were abolished, others such as Yorkshire were split and new counties like Avon and the five metropolitan county councils were created. Patrick Jenkin (Secretary of State 1983–85) abolished the Greater London Council and the metropolitan county councils. Under Michael Heseltine, Secretary of State for the second time between 1990 and 1992, a review into the structure and boundaries of local authorities began.

The Department has reformed local government taxation twice. Under Kenneth Baker (1985–86), Nicholas Ridley (1986–89) and Chris Patten (1989–90) the community charge was devised and introduced. It was subsequently replaced under Michael Heseltine by the council tax.

Peter Walker (1970–72) reformed the housing rebate system by paying the money direct to the householders and not to the local authorities. Between 1979 and 1983 Michael Heseltine developed the policy of selling council houses to their tenants.

Michael Heseltine's second term at the Department saw a major review of the planning system. The move to a development plan-led system in 1991 has given developers and local communities greater certainty about what will and what will not be an acceptable form of development in any given location. The introduction of compulsory publicity for all planning applications has considerably increased the potential for public participation in the planning process.

During Nicholas Ridley's tenure at the Department the water authorities were privatised.

Current Responsibilities
The Department of the Environment has responsibility for local government, planning, housing, new towns, inner city issues, construction, building regulations, environmental protection, water, countryside affairs, property, land holding, and government civil estate management.[7] The Government Car Service, fuel procurement and the London Custody Guard Service also fall within its responsibilities.

The Department is also responsible for the Environmental Protection Group which includes Her Majesty's Inspectorate of Pollution (HMIP). The Inspectorate is responsible for controlling pollution from industrial processes. The Government has announced its intention to set up an Environmental Protection Agency. This will bring together the responsibilities of HMIP and the National Rivers Authority (NRA) which controls water pollution and the waste regulation duties of local government.

The department co-ordinates a wide range of urban regeneration programmes administered by different government departments under the Action for Cities initiative. Action for Cities brings together and gives focus to a comprehensive range of policies designed to promote regeneration in the inner cities. The co-ordination of Government action at the local level is achieved

---

[7]For further information on current responsibilities, see *Planning* (Aspects of Britain: HMSO, 1992), *Conservation* (Aspects of Britain: HMSO, 1993) and *Housing* (Aspects of Britain: HMSO, 1993).

through City Action Teams (CATs), which comprise representatives from all the key Action for Cities departments (in particular the Departments of Employment, Environment and Trade and Industry).

The department is also responsible for the Government's Inner City Task Forces—small teams which aim to improve the targeting of Government help for residents in some of the most deprived urban areas. Legislation currently before Parliament would establish the Urban Regeneration Agency, which is planned to start work later this year. It would be a national body, sponsored by the Department of the Environment, whose main function would be to work in partnership with local authorities and the private sector to bring into productive use derelict, vacant and underused land and buildings.

The Department has four executive agencies: the Queen Elizabeth II Conference Centre, the Buying Agency, the Planning Inspectorate (this serves the Secretaries of State for the Environment and for Wales on appeals and other cases under planning, housing, environment, highways and allied legislation), and the Building Research Establishment.

The Ordnance Survey is a separate department reporting to the Secretary of State for the Environment; it is also an executive agency. It is Britain's national mapping agency and provides official surveying, mapping and associated scientific work covering Britain. It also provides advice to the Overseas Development Administration on mapping and survey work in developing countries. A separate Ordnance Survey covers Northern Ireland.

The Department is also responsible for Property Services Agency Services (PSAS). This organisation, formerly known as the Property Services Agency (PSA), has historically provided and maintained central government property, but has recently undergone reorganisation prior to privatisation. In 1990, the PSA function of Crown landlord was transferred to a new organisation, Property Holdings, a directorate within the Department of the Environment.

At the same time, the remaining part of PSA, called PSA Services, was grouped into four main businesses: PSA Building Management, dealing mainly with maintenance planning and execution; PSA Projects, dealing with project management and design, primarily for new works; PSA Specialist Services, offering specialist technical advice; and PSA International, providing new works and maintenance services to the Ministry of Defence overseas. PSA Specialist Services was combined with PSA Projects six months later, and the combined organisation was subsequently sold to Tarmac Construction Ltd in December 1992. Building Management has been reorganised into five regional businesses, which are expected to be sold during 1993. PSA International will stay in the public sector during its rundown to closure at the end of 1993.

Although the Department of the Environment's responsibilities cover England alone, PSA also has responsibility for Crown properties in Scotland and Wales.

Non-departmental Public Bodies

Executive bodies sponsored by the Department include the Countryside Commission, the Housing Corporation and the Urban Development Corporations. Advisory bodies include the Local Government Commission and the Property Advisory Group. There are three tribunals: the Commons Commissioners, the

Valuation and Community Charge Tribunals and the Rent Assessment Panels.

Office
Since its creation, the Department's headquarters have been based at 2 Marsham Street just south of Parliament. Plans to move are under consideration following the announcement that the existing buildings at Marsham Street will be demolished.

Department of Trade and Industry

Ashdown House, 123 Victoria Street, London SW1E 6RB. Tel: 071-215 5000.

The Department is currently headed by the President of the Board of Trade (Secretary of State for Trade and Industry—see p. 49) who is a member of the Cabinet. At present there are Ministers of State for Energy, and Trade and Industry, and Parliamentary Under-Secretaries of State for Consumer Affairs and Small Firms, Technology, and Corporate Affairs.

History and Development
The Board of Trade grew out of committees of the Privy Council, the first of which was established in 1621. In 1655 Oliver Cromwell created a Committee and Standing Council for Trade and Navigation and, after the restoration in 1660, a Council of Trade and a Council on Foreign Plantations were set up. These two bodies were merged in 1672 but abolished two years later. In 1695 a Board of Trade and Plantations was created, but because most of its responsibilities concerned the old colonial empire this body did not survive the loss of Britain's American colonies. In 1782 the Board

was abolished and its remaining functions given to the Privy Council and the Home Office.

In 1784 William Pitt established a new Committee of the Privy Council on Trade and Plantations as a consultative committee with powers to collect information and provide advice on commercial and colonial issues. In 1786 it was reconstructed and made a permanent part of the machinery of government. The original idea was that the council would be composed of experts in commercial matters who could give authoritative judgements on matters put to them. However, attendance at meetings of the Board declined and from 1820 until the final meeting in 1850 only the president and vice-president attended.

In the nineteenth century the Board of Trade (as the Council on Trade and Plantations came to be known) lost its role in determining commercial policy to the departments concerned with external relations such as the Foreign Office, the Colonial Office, the India Office and the Treasury. But as its influence over the determination of commercial policy declined it acquired responsibility for regulating industry and trade. It obtained the powers of the Railways Commission in 1851, acquired duties under the Merchant Shipping Act of 1854, received responsibility for fisheries policy from the Office of Works in 1866, responsibility for administering the Passenger Acts from the Emigration Commissioners in 1872 and in 1883 became responsible for the administration of the bankruptcy laws.

In the early years of the twentieth century the Board lost many of its functions due to the creation of new departments. In 1903 its responsibility for fisheries was given to the Board of Agriculture and Fisheries. The Board of Trade lost its labour section in 1917 to the Ministry of Labour and in the same year a Ministry of Overseas

Trade acquired responsibility for overseas trade; the Board was given joint responsibility for this ministry. In 1919 most of the Board's powers over railways, tramways, canals and electricity supply and some responsibilities for harbours, piers and docks were given to the Ministry of Transport.

In 1920 responsibility for mines and quarries was acquired from the Home Office when the Mines Department was created. This department was headed by an Under-Secretary at the Board of Trade who was responsible for all the routine work. The President of the Board of Trade retained responsibility for matters involving large issues of policy.

Shipping was relinquished in 1939 to the Ministry of Shipping but in 1941 responsibility for electricity supply was returned following the abolition of the Ministry of War Transport. In 1942 the Board of Trade lost its functions relating to coal, gas, electricity, hydraulic power and petroleum to the new Ministry of Fuel and Power. This ministry also took responsibility for mines and quarries and the Mines Department was abolished.

By 1942 the process of relieving the Board of its responsibilities for the utilities and transport, which had begun in 1916, had been completed. The Board retained a general responsibility for commercial policy and the regulation of many aspects of industry and commerce. In 1946 responsibility for overseas trade was regained when the Department of Overseas Trade was abolished. The Board lost some functions when the Ministry of Materials was created in 1951 but obtained all of that ministry's responsibilities when it was abolished in 1954.

In 1957 the Ministry of Fuel and Power, now renamed the Ministry of Power, took responsibility for iron and steel from the Board of Trade. This new ministry was also made responsible for developing atomic energy as an industrial power source. During the 1960s the Board of Trade lost most of its remaining responsibilities for specific industries to the Ministry of Technology which was created in 1964. In 1969 the Ministry of Power was abolished and its functions given to the Ministry of Technology which was renamed the Ministry of Technology and Power. This new ministry also acquired the Board of Trade's responsibilities for the distribution of industry.

In 1970 the new Conservative Government merged the Ministry of Technology and Power with the Board of Trade to form the Department of Trade and Industry. The new department also acquired responsibility for monopolies, mergers and restrictive practices from the Department of Employment and Productivity. The Department of Trade and Industry did not, however, obtain the Ministry of Technology's former responsibilities for aerospace research, defence and procurement. These functions passed to the newly created Ministry of Aviation Supply. Following the 1974 oil crisis, energy functions were separated and a Department of Energy was created. In 1974 the Labour Government split the Department of Trade and Industry into separate departments covering trade, industry and consumer protection.

In 1979 the incoming Conservative Government abolished the Department of Consumer Protection and gave its functions to the Department of Trade. In 1983 the Departments of Trade and Industry were merged to re-establish a Department of Trade and Industry. Following the abolition of the Department of Energy in 1992 most of its functions were taken over by the Department of Trade and Industry.

The title of President of the Board of Trade was also revived in 1992 when Michael Heseltine, the latest Cabinet minister in charge of the department, announced that he wished to be known by that title rather than as the Secretary of State for Trade and Industry.

Policies and Achievements

Since the creation of the Department of Trade and Industry in 1970 the Department and its successors have enacted much nationalisation and privatisation legislation. John Davies (Secretary of State for Trade and Industry 1970–72) nationalised Rolls Royce but privatised Thomas Cook (a travel company) and State Breweries. Tony Benn (Secretary of State for Industry 1974–75) put public money into three workers' co-operatives, and Eric Varley (1975–79) nationalised the shipbuilding and aircraft industries. Mr Varley also established the National Enterprise Board.

Sir Keith Joseph (Secretary of State for Industry 1979–81) privatised the government's holdings in Ferranti, Fairey Engineering, British Aerospace and Cable and Wireless. Under Patrick Jenkin (1981–83) Amersham International was returned to the private sector. Norman Tebbit (1983–85) privatised Inmos, Jaguar, British Telecom, Yarrow Shipbuilders and Vosper Thornycroft. Paul Channon (1986–87) privatised Swan Hunter, Vickers Shipbuilding and Rolls Royce and Lord Young of Graffham (1987–89) privatised British Steel.

Current Responsibilities

The Department is responsible for international trade policy, including British trade interests in the EC, the General Agreement on Tariffs and Trade (GATT), the United Nations Commission for Trade and Development (UNCTAD), the Organisation for Economic Co-operation and Development (OECD) and other international organisations. The promotion of British exports and assistance to British exporters, and policy in relation to British industry and commerce, including policy towards small firms, regional policy, regional industrial assistance and policy in relation to the Post Office, British Coal and Nuclear Electric plc, also fall within the Department's remit.

Also included are competition policy and consumer protection, including relations with the Office of Fair Trading, the Office of Telecommunications and the Monopolies and Mergers Commission, along with the co-ordination of policy on deregulation, the authorisation of insurance companies and the supervision of insurers. Company legislation is also covered and Companies House has executive agency status within the Department.

Other responsibilities include national and international energy policy and the development of new sources of energy, the oil and gas industries, the electricity supply industry, British Coal, the Atomic Energy Authority and the nuclear power construction industry.[8]

Policy on innovation in industry and in environmental technology, space research, standards, quality and design are also the responsibility of the Department. The Department has five laboratories with executive agency status: the National Weights and Measures Laboratory, Warren Spring Laboratory, the National Physical Laboratory, the National Engineering Laboratory and the Laboratory of the Government Chemist. The Department's other executive agencies are the Insolvency Service, the Radio Communications Agency, the Patent Office and the Accounts Services Agency.

[8]For further information on current policies, see *Energy and Natural Resources* (Aspects of Britain: HMSO, 1992).

The Department's responsibilities extend throughout Britain apart from those relating to the protection of patents and copyrights which cover England, Wales and Scotland only. In addition some of its duties relating to regional industrial assistance are confined to England.

Non-departmental Public Bodies
Executive bodies sponsored by the Department include the National Consumer Council and the National Industry Consumer Councils. Advisory bodies include the Innovation Advisory Board and the British Overseas Trade Board. Tribunals for which the Department is responsible include the Copyright Tribunal, the Insolvency Practitioners' Tribunal, the Persons Hearing Consumer Credit Licensing Appeals Tribunal and the Persons Hearing Estate Agents Tribunal. The Department also sponsors two nationalised industries: the Post Office and British Coal, and a public corporation, Nuclear Electric plc.

Offices
In 1970 the Department of Trade and Industry was established at 1 Victoria Street, the former office of the Board of Trade. When trade and industry were split in 1974 both departments continued to be based at 1 Victoria Street until 1978 when the Department of Industry moved to Ashdown House. In 1983 the unified Department of Trade and Industry was established at 1 Victoria Street. Since 1991 the main address has been Ashdown House.

ECGD (Export Credits Guarantee Department)

2 Exchange Tower, Harbour Exchange Square, London E14 9GS. Tel: 071-512 7000.

ECGD is a separate government department and is headed by a Chief Executive who is responsible to the President of the Board of Trade.

The Department is the Government's official export credit insurer and operates under the Export and Investment Guarantees Act 1991. It was established as the Export Credits Department in 1919 and administered by the Foreign Office and the Board of Trade before becoming an independent department in 1930. In 1953, the functions relating to ECGD were transferred to the President of the Board of Trade.

ECGD helps British exporters by guaranteeing repayment to banks providing export credit finance for project-related goods and services sold on credit terms of two years or more. It also insures private investment overseas.

In 1991 ECGD's short-term credit insurance business was privatised and now operates as NCM Credit Insurance Limited.

Department of Transport

2 Marsham Street, London SW1P 3EB. Tel: 071–276 3000.

The Department is headed by a Secretary of State, who is a member of the Cabinet. At present there are Ministers of State for Public Transport and Aviation and two Parliamentary Under-Secretaries of State.

History and Development

The Ministry of Transport was created in 1919 and was given responsibility for railways, tramways, canals, inland navigation and waterways, light railways, roads, bridges and ferries (including the traffic on them), docks and piers. The Board of Trade's powers relating to the electricity supply industry were also transferred to the new ministry, to be exercised through or by the Electricity Commissioners. The Road Board passed its functions to the Ministry, and was abolished, while substantial powers were transferred from the Board of Trade and the Ministry of Health.

The Ministry's responsibilities were extended by a series of Acts during the 1920s and 1930s; for example, in 1937 responsibility for trunk roads was acquired. In 1941 the Ministry was merged with the Ministry of Shipping to form the Ministry of War Transport and responsibility for electricity supply was returned to the Board of Trade.

In 1946 the Ministry of War Transport was dissolved and its functions given to a new Ministry of Transport. Further change occurred in 1951 when the Conservative Government appointed one minister to cover the offices of Minister of Transport and Minister of Civil Aviation. In 1953 the Government merged transport with civil aviation to create a Ministry of Transport and Civil Aviation; however this arrangement lasted just eight years and in 1959 responsibility for civil aviation was transferred to a Ministry of Civil Aviation.

In 1970 transport was merged with housing and local government to form the Department of the Environment, but in 1976 it was re-established as the Department of Transport.

Policies and Achievements

Since 1945 transport has witnessed many nationalisation and privatisation measures. Alfred Barnes (the Labour Minister of Transport from 1946 to 1951) nationalised the railways, the road haulage industry and the waterways in 1948. In 1953 Alan Lennox

Boyd (Minister of Transport and Civil Aviation 1952–54) privatised part of the road haulage industry. In 1967 Barbara Castle (Labour's Minister of Transport between 1965 and 1968) nationalised the bus industry.

In the 1980s the Conservatives privatised many transport responsibilities including the National Freight Corporation (1982), Associated British Ports (1983), British Rail Hotels (1983), Sealink (1984), the National Bus Company (1986) and British Airways (1986).

Barbara Castle introduced the breathalyser. Harold Watkinson (Minister of Transport and Civil Aviation 1957–59) started work on the London to Birmingham M1 link. Under his successor Ernest Marples (Minister of Transport 1959–64) the M1 was completed and the motorway network extended.

Current Responsibilities

The Department is responsible throughout Britain for land, sea and air transport.[9] Its brief covers airports, domestic and international civil aviation, shipping and the ports, HM coastguard, navigational lights, pilotage, marine pollution and the sponsorship of the bus and rail industries. In England, Scotland and Wales it has oversight of road transport (including vehicle standards, registration and licensing, driver testing and licensing, bus and road-freight licensing and the regulation of taxis and hire cars). In England the Department's remit also extends to the motorways and other trunk roads, road safety and the oversight of local authority transport planning, including the payment of the transport supplementary grant.

[9]For further information on current policies, see *Transport and Communications* (Aspects of Britain: HMSO, 1992).

Six executive agencies perform duties for the Department of Transport. The Driver and Vehicle Licensing Agency (DVLA) is responsible for the registration and licensing of drivers and vehicles and the collection and enforcement of excise duty. The testing and certification of new road and agricultural vehicles is conducted by the Vehicle Certification Agency and the Vehicle Inspectorate is responsible for the annual testing of vehicles. The Driver, Vehicles and Operators Information Technology Directorate provides IT services and the Transport Research Laboratory conducts applied research for the Department and other customers. The Driving Standards Agency promotes road safety in Britain and is responsible for driving tests.

Non-departmental Public Bodies
Executive bodies sponsored by the Department include the Northern Lighthouse Board. Advisory bodies include the Advisory Commission on Historic Wreck Sites and the Disabled Persons Transport Advisory Committee. There is one tribunal: the Traffic Commissioners/Licensing Authorities. The Department is also responsible for three nationalised industries: the British Railways Board, the Civil Aviation Authority and London Regional Transport.

Offices
Since it was re-established as an independent department in 1976, the Department of Transport has been based at 2 Marsham Street, although plans to demolish the building have been announced. From 1961 to 1970 the department was based in St Christopher's House, while between 1940 and 1961 the transport departments were based at Berkeley Square House in Berkeley Square.

Metropole Buildings in Northumberland Avenue was the home of the Ministry of Transport between 1935 and 1940. The original home of the Department from 1919 was in Whitehall Gardens.

Regulatory Bodies

The four regulatory bodies listed below were created to monitor the privatised electricity, gas, telecommunications and water industries. They are headed by Directors General who are appointed by the relevant Secretary of State for a prescribed period of time. The Directors General are each answerable to Parliament in the exercise of their statutory duties.

Office of Electricity Regulation
Hagley House, 83–85 Hagley Road, Birmingham B16 8QG. Tel: 021–456 2100.

The Office of Electricity Regulation (OFFER) is headed by a Director General of Electricity Supply. It is an independent body which monitors the electricity industry and protects electricity customers. The Director General operates under powers given by Parliament in the Electricity Act 1989.

The Director General's key duties are to protect customers and to promote competition in the electricity industry. His other powers and duties include controlling certain prices, settling disputes, issuing licences for generating, transmitting and supplying electricity, investigating complaints and fixing the highest price for which electricity can be re-sold. The Director General has set standards of performance for the companies on the provision of electricity supply services.

There are two Deputy Directors General: one based at the Birmingham headquarters; and one, the Deputy Director General for Scotland, based at OFFER (Scotland) in Glasgow.

OFFER has fourteen regional offices throughout England, Wales and Scotland. There are also fourteen independent electricity consumers' committees made up of representatives from the local community.

In 1992 OFFER published consultation papers, and subsequently reports, on energy efficiency and on metering. Reports were also issued on a range of issues including the profitability and means of remuneration of gas turbines and on whether the electricity supply companies purchase their electricity economically. OFFER also tightened the price control on the National Grid Company's transmission business from nil to three percentage points below the rate of inflation to help keep electricity prices down.

Office of Gas Supply
Stockley House, 130 Wilton Road, London SW1V 1LQ. Tel: 071–828 0898.

The Office of Gas Supply (OFGAS) is headed by a Director General. It was created under the 1986 Gas Act and made responsible for scrutinising the activities of British Gas plc as a public gas supplier. The Office enforces the price formula that determines the average maximum price that British Gas can charge tariff customers, authorises other companies to supply gas through pipes, sets and publishes maximum charges for reselling gas, investigates complaints on issues relevant to its enforcement powers, reviews developments in the gas supply industry, settles the terms on which other suppliers obtain access to British Gas's pipes and produces advice and information for tariff customers. The Office's responsibilities extend throughout Britain.

In 1991 OFGAS intervention led to British Gas announcing price cuts and rebates for 20,000 business customers. In the same year the OFGAS issued an enforcement order against British Gas to prevent a 35 per cent increase in the price of interruptible supplies to large gas users.

Office of Telecommunications
Export House, 50 Ludgate Hill, London EC4M 7JJ.Tel: 071–634 8700.

The Office of Telecommunications (OFTEL) is headed by a Director General. It was created by the Telecommunications Act 1984 and is responsible for supervising telecommunications in Britain. The Office enforces telecommunications licences, approves apparatus, initiates licence amendments and ensures that telecommunications operators comply with the conditions of their licence. OFTEL is charged with promoting and maintaining effective competition and promoting the interests of consumers, purchasers and other users of telecommunications services and apparatus. The Office advises the President of the Board of Trade (the Secretary of State for Trade and Industry) on licensing and other relevant issues and maintains public registers.

The Director General has powers to deal with monopolies and other anti-competitive practices and is responsible for investigating complaints about telecommunications apparatus and services. This includes controlling BT's prices. Its responsibilities extend throughout Britain.

OFTEL sponsors two advisory non-departmental public bodies: the Advisory Committee on Telecommunications for Disabled and Elderly People and the Advisory Committee on Telecommunications for Small Businesses.

Office of Water Services
Centre City Tower, 7 Hill Street, Birmingham B5 4AU. Tel: 021–625 1300.

The Office of Water Services (OFWAT) is headed by a Director General who is appointed by the Secretaries of State for the Environment and for Wales, to whom the Director General reports each year. The Office was established under the Water Act 1989 and is responsible for regulating the economic framework of the water and sewerage industry in England and Wales. OFWAT ensures that the water and sewerage companies comply with their licence terms, regulates the charges the appointed companies make for their services, ensures that these companies have sufficient finance, and protects consumer interests with regard to price and service standards.

OFWAT also compares the performance of the water and sewerage companies and encourages efficiency and economy in the industry. It is responsible for adjudicating in some disputes between the companies and their customers.

The Office has established ten regional customer services committees. They are responsible for the investigation of complaints about the water and sewerage companies, approaching the companies about issues affecting consumer interests and advising the Director of Water Services on consumer matters generally.

OFWAT has encouraged debate on future methods of charging for water. It has supported the selective introduction of metering in areas where water is in short supply and the installation costs of meters are low. In 1994 the Director General will be setting new price limits for the water and sewerage companies. He has suggested that the companies should be able to finance new investment at a lower rate of return through a higher proportion of debt. OFWAT has also pressed for better costing of environmental initiatives so that the impact on customers' payments can be understood before decisions are taken.

Legal Departments

Lord Chancellor's Department

House of Lords, London SW1A OPW. Tel: 071–210 8500.
Trevelyan House, 30 Great Peter Street, London SW1P 2BY. Tel: 071–210 8500.

The Department[10] is headed by the Lord Chancellor, who is a member of the Cabinet. At present a Parliamentary Secretary represents the Department in the House of Commons.

History and Development

The office of Lord Chancellor dates from the eleventh century when the Lord High Chancellor served as the chief of the King's secretaries, the custodian of the royal seal (see p. 17) and the chief royal chaplain. The Lord Chancellor became a trusted royal adviser, especially in issues concerning the exercise of the royal grace—the redress of grievances not provided for by common law.

A litigant had to obtain a writ from the Lord Chancellor before a case could be brought in a royal court. The Chancellor's clerks decided if any form of action was appropriate to the grievance; if none existed the litigant might be able to petition and persuade the Lord Chancellor to create a new one and thus extend the jurisdiction of the royal courts.

---

[10]For further details on Britain's legal departments, see *Britain's Legal Systems* (Aspects of Britain: HMSO, 1993).

By the end of the fifteenth century it was customary for the Lord Chancellor to sit alone to hear petitions and adjudicate on them. The Court of Chancery grew from these origins and was different from the common law courts because it did not have the power to invent new rules but confined its activities to the enforcement of existing rules. The Chancellor did, however, have discretion to consider the merits of the case.

The early Lord Chancellors were clerics such as Thomas à Becket (Lord Chancellor 1154–62) and Cardinal Wolsey (1525–29), but this tradition was broken in 1529 when a lay Lord Chancellor, Sir Thomas More, was appointed. The Lord Chancellor also assumed the role of Speaker of the House of Lords and following the restoration in 1660 this responsibility was enshrined in a Standing Order of Parliament.

Until 1885 the Lord Chancellor was served by a Principal Secretary who handled the appointment of Justices of the Peace, a Secretary of Presentations who dealt with ecclesiastical patronage and several officials who held posts connected with the functions of the Great Seal (p. 17). These secretaries were not permanent officials and left office with the Lord Chancellor.

In 1885 the offices of the Clerk of the Crown in Chancery and the Principal Secretary were combined to form the nucleus of a permanent staff. In the first half of the twentieth century the Lord Chancellor's Office grew from being a small private office into a department as its powers increased. In 1921 the County Courts Department was transferred from the Treasury to the Lord Chancellor's Department. The creation of legal aid in 1947 gave the Lord Chancellor's Department new responsibilities and in 1950 it acquired responsibility from the Home Office for appointing recorders, magistrates (other than in the Duchy of Lancaster), chairmen and deputy chairmen of quarter sessions for the County of London, metropolitan magistrates and stipendiary magistrates.

In 1958 the Lord Chancellor's Department acquired responsibility for the Public Record Office from the Master of the Rolls and in 1965 responsibility for the newly established Law Commission.

In 1971 the Courts Act brought the administration of what had been the assizes and quarter sessions under the control of the Department. As a result of acquiring these new responsibilities it grew from a department with a few officials based in the Palace of Westminster into one employing over 10,000 people.

In April 1992 the Department acquired a second minister when a Parliamentary Secretary was appointed to speak for it in the House of Commons.

Policies and Achievements

Legal aid was created in 1947 during Lord Jowitt's (Lord Chancellor 1945–51) term in office, while Lord Gardiner (1964–70) created the Law Commission. Lord Hailsham (1970–74 and 1979–87) established the Crown Courts in 1971.

Lord Mackay of Clashfern (Lord Chancellor since 1987) removed the Law Society's responsibility for administering legal aid and created a new body, the Legal Aid Board, to perform this task. Lord Mackay has also introduced legislation which is aimed at extending rights of audience in the courts enjoyed by solicitors and established the Legal Services Ombudsman and the Lord Chancellor's Advisory Committee on Legal Education and Conduct.

Robert Walpole, the first Earl of Orford, was chief minister from 1721 to 1742 and is often considered to have been Britain's first Prime Minister.

William Gladstone, Prime Minister for four terms (1868–74, 1880–85, 1886, 1892–94) addressing the House of Commons.

The Imperial War Cabinet in 1917. It included representatives from a number of countries which are now part of the Commonwealth.

Lord Callaghan, Prime Minister 1976–79, who unusually served in three of the most senior offices of state – as Chancellor of the Exchequer, Home Secretary and Foreign Secretary – before becoming Prime Minister.

Treasury Chambers, Parliament Street, London, the home of Her Majesty's Treasury (see pp. 21–7).

Whitehall, London, is now synonymous with Britain's central government. It remains the home of many of the largest government departments.

St. Andrew's House, Edinburgh, the headquarters of the Scottish Office (see pp. 119–24).

Kenneth Clarke, Home Secretary from April 1992 to May 1993, meeting the Indian Minister for Home Affairs for the signing of an extradition treaty.

A COI Network Services office in Newcastle.

Current Responsibilities

The Lord Chancellor's Department is responsible for promoting the reform of civil law and civil court procedure; the Home Office has important responsibilities for the criminal law (p. 76). The Lord Chancellor is personally responsible for advising the Crown (and the Prime Minister) on the appointment of judges and appoints some other officials himself. He receives advice from the department about these appointments. Other responsibilities include the administration of the Supreme Court (the Court of Appeal, the High Court and the Crown Court), the county courts and the magistrates courts in England and Wales; and the Northern Ireland Court Service, some other courts, tribunals and the Council on Tribunals.

The appointment of Masters and Registrars of the High Court and District and County Court district judges and magistrates also come within its remit.

The Department has responsibility for legal aid and as custodian of the Great Seal of the Realm the Lord Chancellor is responsible for ensuring that letters patent and other formal documents are passed in the correct form. This latter work is conducted at the Lord Chancellor's direction in the Office of the Clerk of the Crown in Chancery.

The Department advises the Lord Chancellor on his responsibility for maintaining the national archives, a task performed by the Public Record Office (an executive agency). The Department is responsible for the Land Registry (also an executive agency) which keeps a record of land ownership, the Public Trust Office and the Official Solicitor's Department; it also considers and provides policy advice on aspects of private international law. The Legal

Services Ombudsman is independent of the Department but reports to the Lord Chancellor.

As ex-officio Speaker of the House of Lords, the Lord Chancellor chairs debates in that House and as head of the judiciary occasionally serves as a judge as part of the Judicial Committee of the House of Lords (or of the Appellate Committee of the Privy Council).

Non-departmental Public Bodies
The Department sponsors one executive body: the Legal Aid Board. Advisory bodies include the Council on Tribunals, the Law Commission, the Statute Law Committee, the Advisory Council on Public Records and the Crown Court Rule Committee. There are six tribunals: the Transport Tribunal, the Value Added Tax Tribunal, the Pensions Appeal Tribunal, the Lands Tribunal and the two immigration appellate systems.

Offices
The Lord Chancellor has been based at the Palace of Westminster since it was re-built by Sir Charles Barry following the fire of 1834 that destroyed most of the old palace. Most of the administrative staff are based in Trevelyan House.

Legal Secretariat to the Law Officers

Attorney General's Chambers, 9 Buckingham Gate, London SW1E 6JP. Tel: 071–828 7155.

This department serves the Attorney General, who is assisted by the Solicitor General.

The Office of Attorney General is a very old one. As far back as the thirteenth century, the King's Attorney and the King's Sergeant were responsible for maintaining the Sovereign's interests before the courts. Over the years, the names and roles of these officers have changed. Today the Law Officers are the Attorney General and his deputy the Solicitor General.

Despite the long history of the offices of Attorney General and Solicitor General it was only in 1893 that any provision was made for a department of clerical staff to assist the Law Officers in the exercise of their functions. Until then they had been expected to continue as practising barristers and undertake the business of government from their chambers. The early years of the twentieth century brought a large increase in the workload of the Law Officers and resulted in the creation of the post of Legal Secretary to head the Law Officers' Department. As the volume and variety of work dealt with by the departments has grown, so too has the number of staff. With a change of name in 1989 to the Legal Secretariat to the Law Officers the department now has a staff of ten lawyers to assist the Legal Secretary. Support and administrative staff bring the total number within the department to 27.

The Attorney General, assisted by the Solicitor General, is the chief legal adviser to the Government and is ultimately responsible for all Crown litigation both at home and in international courts. He superintends the Crown Prosecution Service, the Serious Fraud Office, and the Treasury Solicitor's Department—as well as his own department. In addition he has overall responsibility for the work of the Government Legal Service as a whole. He is also the Attorney General for Northern Ireland.

As well as the general duties imposed by his status as adviser to the Government, the Attorney General has many specific responsibilities in both the civil and criminal fields. Relator actions, such as suits to compel the performance of some statutory duties by public bodies, can only be brought with his consent; he is also responsible for making applications to the court to restrain the activities of vexatious litigants and for supervising the activities of the Queen's Proctor, an officer with certain functions relating to the divorce laws. Although not responsible for charity law, the Attorney General is generally a necessary party to any litigation in which the objects of a charity need to be separately represented. He must advise the Sovereign on the disposal of gifts given to charity where no specific charity has been named. His duties to advise the Sovereign also include the granting of Royal Charters and advice in peerage cases. He acts as guardian of the public interest to bring contempt proceedings where appropriate to protect the integrity of the administration of justice.

The Attorney General's responsibilities in the criminal field are just as wide ranging. In addition to his superintendence of the Crown Prosecution Service and the Serious Fraud Office there are numerous offences that can be prosecuted only with his consent. He also has the power to stay any proceedings on indictment—whoever the prosecutor may be. Where there has been an acquittal in a criminal case to the Court of Appeal, he also has the power to refer to the Court of Appeal a sentence imposed for an indictable offence which he considers to be unduly lenient, to allow the court to consider increasing that sentence. He has a range of additional responsibilities both under statute and at common law.

The Legal Secretariat is responsible for evaluating any application made to the Law Officers, preparing any briefing, advising, and if appropriate, ensuring that any action consequent to the decision is carried out.

HM Procurator General and Treasury Solicitor's Department

Queen Anne's Chambers, 28 Broadway, London SWIH 9JS. Tel: 071–210 3000.

This non-ministerial department is headed by the Procurator General and Treasury Solicitor; ministerial responsibility for its actions lies with the Attorney General (p. 67). The office of Treasury Solicitor dates from the seventeenth century when it was charged with providing the Treasury with legal advice. In 1685 the Treasury Solicitor was made responsible for political prosecutions, but lost these functions in 1696. In 1842 the services provided by this office were made available to the other departments.

Since 1876 the post of Treasury Solicitor has been held in conjunction with the ancient office of Procurator General. The latter office was once responsible for the performance of many functions under ecclesiastical, Admiralty and prerogative law but is now largely confined to duties relating to the marriage and divorce laws. The post of Treasury Solicitor was held by the Director of Public Prosecutions from 1884 to 1908 when the Prosecution of Offences Act separated the offices once more (see p. 70).

The office of HM Procurator General and Treasury Solicitor, whose remit extends throughout England and Wales, provides legal services for many government departments. Departments without their own lawyers are given legal advice, and both they and many other departments are provided with litigation services. Government Property Lawyers, an executive agency, provides conveyancing and lands advisory services to government departments and other public bodies. The Department's duties include instructing Parliamentary Counsel on Bills, drafting subordinate legislation, providing advice on the application and interpretation of the law and representing departments in court. The department also administers the estates of people who die intestate and without any known relatives, and handles the outstanding property rights of dissolved companies.

Crown Prosecution Service

4–12 Queen Anne's Gate, London SW1H 9AZ. Tel: 071–273 8152.

The head of the Crown Prosecution Service (CPS) is the Director of Public Prosecutions (DPP), who discharges his or her functions under the superintendence of the Attorney General. The Crown Prosecution Service is responsible for the prosecution of almost all criminal cases resulting from police investigations in England and Wales.

The office of DPP was created by the Prosecution of Offences Act 1879 and existed for over a hundred years before the CPS came into being. Sir Augustus Stephenson (DPP 1884–94) and Hamilton Cuffe (1894–1908) held the office in conjunction with the post of Treasury Solicitor (see p. 69). From 1880 to 1986 the DPP handled only the relatively small number of cases that were defined as being important or difficult, or in which his intervention was required for any other reason (the number of cases rose from about 500 in 1880 to about 18,000 in 1978). The prosecution of most other cases was the responsibility of the police. By 1986 the number of lawyers in the DPP's London-based department had risen from one to seventy.

The Crown Prosecution Service was created by the Prosecution of Offences Act 1985, following recommendations made by the Royal Commission on Criminal Procedure. It became operational throughout England and Wales by October 1986. The DPP was made head of this department, which was staffed initially with some 1,700 lawyers and over 2,000 non-lawyers (now there are 2,000 lawyers and over 4,000 non-lawyers). The CPS prosecutes about 1.6 million cases a year.

The formation of the CPS meant that the processes of the investigation and prosecution of crime were separated. The role of the CPS is to review the evidence gathered by the police and decide, first, whether there is sufficient evidence for a realistic prospect of conviction and secondly, whether the public interest requires a prosecution. The police do not have to consult the CPS before charging (although they often do) but the decision on whether to continue with the prosecution rests with the CPS.

From October 1993 the CPS will be divided into 13 areas covering England and Wales (at present there are 31 areas). Each area is headed by a Chief Crown Prosecutor. The CPS headquarters is based in London.

Serious Fraud Office

Elm House, 10–16 Elm Street, London WC1X OBJ. Tel: 071–239 7272.

The head of the Serious Fraud Office (SFO) is the Director of Serious Fraud Office, who discharges his or her functions under the superintendence of the Attorney General. Ministerial responsibility for the department lies with the Attorney General. The SFO investigates and prosecutes the most complex and serious fraud cases in England, Wales and Northern Ireland.

The SFO began operations in April 1988 following recommendations made by the Fraud Trials Committee chaired by Lord Roskill that there was a need for a new, unified organisation responsible for the detection, investigation and prosecution of serious fraud cases. The Office and its powers were created under the Criminal Justice Act 1987.

The SFO handles approximately 60 cases at any one time. Referrals come from, among others, the police, other government departments and regulatory bodies. Before a case is accepted, one of the following criteria must be satisfied: either the facts and/or law are complex, or there is great public interest or concern. In judging referrals, account is taken of the need to use the Office's powers created under section 2 of the Criminal Justice Act 1987, and normally whether the alleged fraud exceeds £5 million.

When a case is accepted, a case team of lawyers, accountants, police officers and support staff is appointed. The team is headed by a senior lawyer, who as case controller is responsible for ensuring an expeditious and effective investigation and for any ensuing prosecution.

Lord Advocate's Department

Fielden House, 10 Great College Street, London SW1P 3SL. Tel 071–276 3000.

The Lord Advocate and the Solicitor General for Scotland are the Law Officers of the Crown for Scotland and the chief legal advisers to the Government in Scottish questions. Members of the

Department assist them in these matters and act as legal advisers on Scottish questions to certain government departments. Before the union with England in 1707 the Lord Advocate, as an Officer of State and a member of the Privy Council, took part in the political as well as the legal aspect of government. Following the Act of Union the Lord Advocate emerged as virtually the only Scottish minister in the eighteenth and nineteenth centuries and responsibilities once performed by other Scottish officials were transferred to him as the Crown's principal law officer in Scotland. He handled the greater part of the Scottish business in the House of Commons. The influence of the post was heavily dependent on the character and prestige of the incumbent (see p. 119).

There was, however, widespread discontent with the Lord Advocate's political role and in 1885 a Secretary for Scotland was appointed (see p. 120). The Secretary for Scotland, or Secretary of State for Scotland—as the post was renamed in 1926—became the principal political figure in Scotland and the Lord Advocate's office became confined to a legal role.

The Department assists the Scottish Law Officers and advises several government departments on Scottish law. Members of the Department act as Scottish Parliamentary Counsel and draft government legislation that relates wholly or mainly to Scotland and adapts other legislation to Scottish requirements.

Crown Office

5–7 Regent Road, Edinburgh ER7 5BL. Tel: 031–557 3800.

The Lord Advocate is responsible for the prosecution of all crime in Scotland. The function is discharged centrally through the Crown Office and at local level through procurators fiscal, who also direct the police in the investigation of crime and investigate all sudden or suspicious deaths. The Crown Office is the headquarters of the Procurator Fiscal Service.

All prosecutions in the High Court of Justiciary (which deals with the most serious crime) are conducted by Crown Counsel, who are based at the Crown Office, while prosecutions in the Sheriff and Jury, Sheriff Summary and District Courts are conducted by members of the Procurator Fiscal Service.

Social Departments

The Home Office

50 Queen Anne's Gate, London SW1H 9AT. Tel: 071–273 3000.

The Home Office is headed by the Secretary of State for the Home Department, who is a member of the Cabinet. The department also currently has three Ministers of State and a Parliamentary Under-Secretary of State.

History and Development

Although it originated from the office of the Sovereign's Secretary, the Home Office was created in its modern form in 1782 when the work of the two existing Secretaries of State was rationalised. Before then the Northern and Southern Secretaries (as they were styled—see p. 5) had divided foreign and domestic business between them. Afterwards, domestic business became the sole concern of the minister who became known as the Home Secretary, and foreign matters became the responsibility of the Foreign Secretary.

In 1782 domestic matters included not only the internal government of Great Britain as a whole but also responsibility for that of Ireland, the Channel Islands, and the colonies. (Also included initially were relations with the Barbary States and former Board of Trade business.) The Home Office's work was then very limited in comparison with its future responsibilities. It had a staff of under

20 and its work consisted of considering petitions for pardons, granting free pardons, commuting sentences, dealing with petitions to the King on all kinds of subjects, granting army commissions, transportation, issuing directions for troop movements in Great Britain and Ireland, and correspondence with the Lord Lieutenant of Ireland, the governors of the colonies, the Isle of Man, the Channel Islands, and the Lord Advocate and other Scottish authorities.

Since 1782 the history of the Home Office has involved developing existing, latent and—sometimes—transferred responsibilities as society became more complex, while ceding responsibilities to new government departments as it became convenient to create them. An important factor was that statute law came to play an increasingly significant role as the British state was modernised. For example, the Gaol Act of 1823 sought to improve the management of prisons; the 1835 Act introduced government inspection, and the 1877 Act brought local prisons under central management. The Metropolitan Police were established by the Peel Act of 1829. Legislation for provincial forces followed in 1830, 1839, 1840 and 1856 when establishing such forces became obligatory. Factory inspection began in 1833 and was extended to the mines in 1842. Criminal justice legislation was introduced with increasing frequency to reform the criminal law (Sir Robert Peel passed eight such Acts), to regulate and then end transportation, and to construct both the prisons and the system of penal servitude which ultimately replaced it.

Home Secretaries have always faced a wide range of duties. During the nineteenth century, Irish affairs were a constant preoccupation in addition to concern for maintaining the peace in Britain. In addition to those issues already mentioned the Home

Office was responsible for the poor law, health and local government legislation until 1871, as well as for roads, fisheries, trade union law, and workmen's compensation. It assumed statutory responsibilities for explosives in 1875 and for cruelty to animals in 1876. Similarly, the law relating to citizenship and immigration was developed variously in the Acts of 1844, 1870 and 1905. In the early part of this century, the Home Office became responsible for civil aviation; in 1951 the Home Secretary was designated (until 1957) as the Minister for Welsh affairs; and in 1974, with the abolition of the Ministry of Post and Telecommunications, the Home Office gained responsibility for broadcasting until that in turn passed to the new Department of National Heritage in 1992. War and the threat of war during the twentieth century led to the development of civil defence and the fire service.

Throughout its history the Home Office's functions have changed following the creation of new departments. The outbreak of war in 1793 led to the establishment of a Ministry of War the following year. This relieved the Home Office of its responsibility for the Army, although its direct law and order powers in relation to the movement of troops within Britain were retained until the creation of the War Department in 1855. In 1801 the Ministry of War took the Home Office's responsibility for colonies, while in 1858 its responsibility for India was transferred to the India Office. In 1871 the newly created Local Government Board took charge of responsibility for local government and the poor laws.

In 1885 the Scottish Office was established. It acquired the Home Office's responsibility for Scottish criminal business and all of the Home Secretary's Scottish functions that could be separated from their application in England and Wales. The creation of the Board of Agriculture in 1899 deprived the Home Secretary of further duties; and responsibility for civil aviation passed to the Air Ministry in 1919, while responsibility for mines was surrendered to the Mines Department when it was formed in 1920. In 1940 Home Office powers under the Factory Acts were given to the Ministry of Labour and National Service. Responsibility for children passed to the Department of Health in 1970 and for the running of magistrates' courts to the Lord Chancellor's Department in 1992. Conversely, passports were taken over from the Foreign Office in 1984.

Policies and Achievements

In the nineteenth century the Home Office was responsible for many social reforms. Sir Robert Peel (Home Secretary 1822–27 and 1828–30) reformed the system of criminal law and founded the modern police service; Lord Palmerston (1852–55) secured the passage of the first Reformatory Schools Act in 1854; while Sir George Grey, three times Home Secretary for a total of over 13 years between 1846 and 1866, introduced the Police Act 1856; and Herbert Gladstone (Home Secretary 1905–10) helped—originally as Parliamentary Under-Secretary—initiate a process of prison reform which created new ways of handling youths in the Borstal system and ultimately did much to improve prison life.

More recently immigration and the social issues surrounding it have received a good deal of attention. R. A. Butler (Home Secretary 1957–62) extended immigration control to Commonwealth citizens. James Callaghan (1967–70) and Reginald Maudling (1970–72) further strengthened the control. William Whitelaw (1979–83) reformed British citizenship law. Both Roy Jenkins (1965–67 and 1974–76) and James Callaghan (1967–70) introduced measures to combat racial discrimination and encourage equal opportunities by establishing the Race Relations Board, its successor the Commission for Racial Equality, and the Equal Opportunities Commission.

Since the end of the second world war, criminal justice has remained the most frequent object of legislation. The Criminal Justice Act 1948 (under Chuter Ede, Home Secretary 1945–51) reformed the powers of the courts and abolished corporal punishment; R. A. Butler's 1961 Act continued the process; capital punishment was abolished in 1965; and Roy Jenkins' Act of 1967 introduced parole. Important changes in criminal law were also contained in the Criminal Law Act 1977 (Merlyn Rees, 1976–79), in the Police and Criminal Evidence Act 1984 and the Prosecution of Offences Act 1985 (under Leon Brittan, Home Secretary 1983–85), and in the Criminal Justice Acts of 1988 (under Douglas Hurd, 1985–89) and 1991 (under Kenneth Baker, 1990–92).

The Home Office instituted several broadcasting reforms when it was responsible for broadcasting policy. William Whitelaw (1979–83) created Channel 4 in 1982. The regulation of independent television and radio was overhauled under Douglas Hurd and David Waddington (1989–90).

Current Responsibilities

The Home Office is responsible for the administration of justice, the police, the criminal law and the treatment of offenders, including the prison service and probation service. It also has responsibility for nationality issues, passport matters and immigration. Community relations, race relations, some public safety issues and the fire and civil emergency services also fall within the department's remit.

The Home Secretary is the link between the Queen and the public and exercises powers on her behalf such as the royal pardon. Petitions to the Queen, the granting of scientific licences for experiments involving animals, charitable collections, scrutiny of local authority by-laws and electoral arrangements are covered by the Home Office.

The department is responsible for dangerous drugs and poisons, shops legislation, cremations, burials and exhumations, marriage, the licensing of theatres and cinemas, the extradition of criminals, firearms, liquor licensing, gaming, lotteries, ceremonial and formal matters connected with honours and the co-ordination of government activities relating to the voluntary social services.

In most matters the Home Office's responsibilities are confined to England and Wales. However the Office is also responsible for gaming policy in Scotland and its authority over immigration, nationality, race relations issues and royal matters extends throughout Britain. The Home Office handles relations with the Channel Islands and the Isle of Man.

Four executive agencies are the responsibility of the Home Office: the Forensic Science Service, HM Prison Service, the United Kingdom Passport Agency and the Fire Service College. The last agency provides training in the fire and rescue services and is also involved in research and consultancy on fire prevention.

Non-departmental Public Bodies
Executive bodies sponsored by the department include the Commission for Racial Equality, the Office of Data Protection Registrar and the Police Complaints Authority. Advisory bodies

include the Parole Board and the Parliamentary Boundary
Commission for England. Tribunals include the Criminal Injuries
Compensation Board.

Offices
When the Board of Trade was abolished in 1782 the Home Office
acquired its former offices in Whitehall. Following the re-
establishment of the Board in 1786 the Home Office moved to the
Old Tennis Court complex, also in Whitehall. In 1875 the head-
quarters of the Home Office were moved into a new building in
Whitehall next to the Colonial Office and the Local Government
Office, near to the site of the Cenotaph.

The construction of this building, designed by Gilbert Scott
in the classical style, enabled all the parts of the Home Office to be
unified at one site for a time. Scott's building served as the department's headquarters until 1977 when the Home Office moved to its
present address at Queen Anne's Gate.

Department for Education

Sanctuary Buildings, Great Smith Street, London SW1P 3BT.
Tel: 071–925 5000.

This department is headed by a Secretary of State, who is a mem-
ber of the Cabinet. At present there is a Minister of State, a
Parliamentary Under-Secretary of State for Higher and Further
Education and a Parliamentary Under-Secretary of State for
Schools.

History and Development

Government involvement in the modern school system in England and Wales began in the first half of the nineteenth century. In 1833 the first grants of public money towards the cost of education were made and an Education Committee of the Privy Council was created in 1839. The 1870 Elementary Education Act created a national network of schools and in 1873 children of parents receiving poor relief were forced to attend. In 1880 attendance was made compulsory for all children between five and ten and in 1891 an Act made all elementary education free. In 1899 the Committee was merged with the Science and Art Department to become the Board of Education and the school-leaving age was increased to 12. The Board never met and in practice all its powers were vested in the President. The Technical Education Act 1889 made technical education the responsibility of the new local authorities. In 1903 the local authorities became responsible for all elementary, secondary and technical education and voluntary schools and the School Boards were dissolved.

In 1944 the Board of Education was renamed the Ministry of Education and its President became the Minister for Education. The 1944 Education Act gave the Minister for Education many new powers. The Minister acquired a duty to supervise standards in independent schools and obtained powers to supervise, control and direct the local education authorities whose responsibilities were increased by the Act.

In 1964 the Conservative administration combined the Office of the Minister for Science with the Ministry of Education to form the Department of Education and Science. The inclusion of the Office of the Minister for Science gave the Department some civil science functions. The 1964 reorganisation also returned responsibility for the financing of the universities which the Ministry of Education had last exercised in 1919. The Department was given control of financial assistance to the arts and the library service in 1965. In 1983 the Office of Arts and Libraries was separated from the Department; in 1992 these matters were acquired by the Department of National Heritage.

The Department of Education and Science lost many of its responsibilities in Wales to the Welsh Office in the 1970s and in 1992 was renamed the Department for Education following the transfer of its responsibilities for science to the Office of Public Service and Science. The Department of Education and Science had responsibility for sport between 1964 and 1970 and again between 1990 and 1992 after which it passed to the Department of National Heritage.

Policies and Achievements

H.A.L. Fisher (President of the Board of Education 1916–22) raised the school-leaving age to 14, introduced free secondary-school places and established a national system for determining teachers' pay.

The 1944 Education Act, which was enacted under R.A. Butler (President of the Board of Education 1941–44 and Minister of Education 1944–45), created a tripartite system of grammar, technical and secondary modern schools, and abolished the payment of fees in local authority schools.

Ellen Wilkinson (1945–47) introduced free school meals in all local education authorities. The school-leaving age was raised to 15 under George Tomlinson (1947–51) in 1947, and to 16 in 1973 under Margaret Thatcher (Secretary of State for Education and Science 1970–74). During the 1960s and 1970s the Department played a key role in the establishment of many comprehensive schools which replaced the tripartite system in most areas.

Under Kenneth Baker (1986–89) the Department introduced the Education Reform Act of 1988. This established national tests in schools, gave schools the right to opt out of local authority control and achieve grant-maintained status, and created city technology colleges.

Following the publication of the Robbins Report in 1963 the number of students in higher education was increased and many new universities were created. In the late 1960s polytechnics were established and the Open University was created in 1969. In 1992 the Government abolished the distinction between the polytechnics and the universities.

Current Responsibilities

The Department for Education has overall responsibility for formulating and promoting policies for education in England and is also responsible for the Government's relations with the universities in England, Scotland and Wales.[11]

The Department's brief covers the broad allocation of educational resources, the formulation of national education policies, capital building programmes for schools and other educational institutions, the supply, training and superannuation of teachers, and basic educational standards. Since the passage of the Education Reform Act 1988 the Department has become involved in funding schools. Schools now have the right to apply for grant-maintained status, opt out of local authority control and receive their funds direct from the Department.

[11]For further information on current policies, see *Education* (Aspects of Britain: HMSO, 1993).

The Teachers' Superannuation Scheme is handled by the Teachers' Pensions Agency, which is an executive agency.

Non-departmental Public Bodies
Executive bodies sponsored by the Department include the Higher Education Funding Council for England, the National Curriculum Council and the School Examination and Assessment Council. The Government plans to replace the National Curriculum Council and the School Examinations and Assessment Council with the School Curriculum and Assessment Authority and the Funding Agency for Schools later in 1993. Advisory bodies include the Open University Visiting Committee.

Offices
In 1944 the Ministry of Education was established at Belgrave Square on the site of the former Board of Education; it moved to Curzon Street in 1948. In 1964 the Department of Education and Science was established at Curzon Street and Richmond Terrace in Whitehall where the former Office of the Minister for Science had been located. After a few months the Department's headquarters were unified at the Curzon Street site. In 1972 the Department moved to Elizabeth House in York Road next to Waterloo Station before moving to its present address in 1992.

Office for Standards in Education (OFSTED)

Elizabeth House, York Road, London SE1 7PH. Tel: 071–925 6773.

OFSTED was established in September 1992 and is headed by Her Majesty's Chief Inspector of Schools in England. The Office is responsible for monitoring standards in English schools and regulating the work of independent registered schools inspectors.

Department of Health

Richmond House, 79 Whitehall, London SW1A 2NS. Tel: 071–210 3000.

The Department of Health is headed by a Secretary of State, who is a member of the Cabinet. There are also currently a Minister of State and three Parliamentary Under-Secretaries of State.

History and Development

The Ministry of Health Act 1919 established a Ministry of Health with responsibilities relating to health and local government in England and Wales. The Act transferred all the powers of the Local Government Board (see p. 40), the Insurance Commission and the Welsh Insurance Commission to the Ministry. The Health Ministry also received powers of the Board of Education relating to the health of expectant mothers, children under five and young persons, and functions of the Privy Council in relation to midwives in England and Wales.

The Department's planning functions were lost when the Ministry of Works and Planning was created in 1942, while responsibilities for pensions and national insurance passed to the Ministry of National Insurance in 1945. In 1948 the Ministry of Health became responsible for the new National Health Service (NHS) and relinquished responsibility for some of its poor law functions to the National Assistance Board.

In 1951 health was split from housing and local government when the functions relating to local government rating and valuation, housing, rent control, burials and coast protection were given to the new Ministry of Housing and Local Government. The Department's functions in Wales were lost to the Welsh Office in 1968.

In 1964 the incoming Labour Government gave a non-departmental Cabinet minister the job of co-ordinating the social services. In 1968 the then co-ordinating minister, Richard Crossman, became the Secretary of State for Social Services when the Ministries of Health and Social Security combined to form the Department of Health and Social Security. This arrangement lasted until 1988 when the Conservative Government split the department into a Department of Health and a Department of Social Security, each represented in the Cabinet.

Policies and Achievements

The Ministry of Health established the NHS in 1948, under Aneurin Bevan (Minister of Health 1945–51) with the objective of providing the population with access to free health care.

Kenneth Clarke (Secretary of State for Health 1988–90) introduced the purchaser/provider split and contracting into the NHS, set up the NHS Trusts and GP fund-holding practices and set out a framework and agenda for developing community care. Virginia Bottomley (1992–) has set strategic targets for improvements in a range of key areas of health.

Current Responsibilities

The Department of Health is responsible for public health, for the NHS in England and for personal social services run by English local authorities which provide help for the elderly, the disabled, young people, and children in need of care.[12] The Department's functions also extend to food safety, welfare foods, regulation of medical devices and equipment, the medical treatment of war pensioners and, under the Civil Defence Act 1948, to the ambulance and emergency-aid services and to international aspects of health. It acts as Britain's representative at the World Health Organisation (WHO) and other international organisations, and makes reciprocal health agreements with other countries.

An executive agency, the Medicines Control Agency, is responsible for licensing medicines, dental and surgical products, conducting clinical trials, reviewing the performance of drugs, labelling and the production of patient-information leaflets. It is also responsible for licensing and inspecting manufacturers and wholesale dealers. The NHS Agency advises the Department and the NHS on the management of the estate and offers consultancy services to health authorities and trusts. A third agency, NHS Pensions, is responsible for the NHS Superannuation Scheme.

The Department's responsibilities for the NHS, personal social services and public health are confined to England. In its international role, however, the Department speaks and negotiates on behalf of Britain.

Non-departmental Public Bodies

Executive bodies sponsored by the department include the National Radiological Protection Board, the Medical Practices Committee and the Public Health Laboratory Services Board. Advisory bodies include the Standing Medical Advisory

[12]For further information on current policies, see *Social Welfare* (Aspects of Britain: HMSO, 1993).

Committee, the Joint Committee on Vaccination and Communication, the Health Advisory Service and the Committee on Safety of Medicines. There are three tribunals: the Mental Health Review Tribunal, the National Health Service Tribunal, and the Registered Home Tribunals.

Offices

The Department of Health moved to its present address in Richmond House in 1988. Between 1963 and 1988 the Department was run from Alexander Fleming House in the Elephant and Castle in south London where it retains a substantial office. The Ministry of Health was based in Savile Row from 1951 to 1963; its original home was in Whitehall.

Office of Population Censuses and Surveys

St Catherine's House, 10 Kingsway, London WC2B 6JP. Tel: 071–242 0262.

This non-ministerial office is headed by a Director who is also Registrar General for England and Wales. The Office was created in 1970 by the merger of the General Register Office and the Government Social Survey Department.

The department administers the law on marriages, and controls the registration of births, marriages and deaths. It also conducts the census of the population and provides a wide range of important demographic and health statistics.

Social surveys are conducted for other government departments and public bodies and the Office maintains the National

Health Service Central Register for the Department of Health and the Welsh Office at Southport in Merseyside.

The index of birth, marriage and death registration certificates are kept at St Catherine's House and are available for inspection by the public between 08.30 and 16.30 on weekdays. The department also maintains the Adopted Children's Register and the Adoption Contact Register at its Southport office.

The Office conducts social surveys for departments with responsibilities in any country of Britain. Its other duties are confined to England and Wales.

Department of Social Security

Richmond House, 79 Whitehall, London SW1A 2NS. Tel: 071–210 3000.

The Department is headed by a Secretary of State who is a member of the Cabinet. There is at present a Minister of State with responsibility for disabled people, and three Parliamentary Under-Secretaries of State.

History and Development

As early as the end of the sixteenth century the principle of public responsibility for the relief of poverty was accepted in Britain. In 1601 the Poor Law was passed in England and Wales. A similar Act had been passed in Scotland in 1579. It was administered at parish level by the Guardians of the Poor Law and provided *ad hoc* payments or money in kind or accommodation in a workhouse to the poorest citizens. Medical attention was available under the Poor Law and hospitals were established in some areas. In 1834 a central board was created to administer the system and in 1847 the board was placed under ministerial control. In 1871 the Poor Law Board acquired the local government functions of the Home Office and some duties from the Board of Public Health and was renamed the Local Government Board.

By 1900 a strong reaction had begun against the form and spirit of the Poor Law, and new methods of public provision began to appear. In 1908 the Liberal Government introduced a scheme for the payment of non-contributory old age pensions to people over 70 of limited means. In 1911 it introduced two contributory insurance schemes. An Unemployment Insurance Scheme was established for workers in some jobs. Responsibility for administration was given to the Board of Trade and passed to the newly created Ministry of Labour in 1916 (see p. 36). The National Insurance Act 1911, which covered all manual and lower-paid non-manual workers, provided medical attention and money benefits to those who were sick and unable to work. It also created a limited system of maternity benefits. The system was administered by friendly societies, medical aid societies, industrial assurance companies and trade unions.

The Ministry of Pensions was established in 1916 to take over the duties of the Army Council, the Admiralty and the Commissioners of Chelsea Hospital in relation to war pensions. In 1929 the local Poor Law Boards, which still administered the Poor Law scheme, were abolished and their powers transferred to public assistance committees of the county and county borough councils.

In 1934 the Government established an Unemployment Assistance Board to administer a new benefits scheme for the unemployed. This took responsibility for individual benefit decisions while the Ministry of Labour was responsible for issues of policy. In 1940 the Board acquired responsibility for paying additional benefits to pensioners from the local public assistance committees and was renamed the Assistance Board.

The Ministry of National Insurance was created in 1944 following recommendations made in the Beveridge Report (1942), which established a comprehensive system of social insurance. In 1945 the Ministry obtained the powers and duties of the Ministry of Health and the Scottish Office in relation to health insurance and pensions, of the Ministry of Labour and National Service in relation to unemployment insurance and assistance, and of the Home Office with regard to workers' compensation.

Sir William (later Lord) Beveridge had suggested that the Assistance Board lose its independence; however the Government disagreed and it did not become part of the Ministry of National Insurance. Instead the Board retained all its existing functions and acquired the pensions work of the Board of Customs and Excise and the remaining Poor Law work of the local authorities. By 1947 the Assistance Board was responsible for all non-contributory pensions and *ad hoc* financial aid. In the following year it acquired the functions of the public assistance committees and was renamed the National Assistance Board.

In 1953 the Ministry of Pensions was amalgamated with the Ministry of National Insurance, and its health functions passed to the Ministry of Health and the Scottish Office. In 1966 responsibility for contributory and non-contributory benefits was united in the same department when the Ministry of Pensions and National Insurance was merged with the National Assistance Board to form the Ministry of Social Security.

A further merger occurred in 1968 when the Ministry of Social Security was amalgamated with the Ministry of Health to form the Department of Health and Social Security; this change was reversed in 1988 when separate departments for Health and for Social Security were created.

Policies and Achievements
In 1966 Margaret Herbison, the first Minister of Social Security, replaced national assistance with supplementary benefits. Barbara Castle (Secretary of State for Social Services 1974–76) introduced child benefit and David Ennals (1976–79) established the state earnings related pensions scheme (SERPS).

A major reform of the system was conducted by Sir Norman Fowler (1981–87). Sir Norman introduced personal pensions, created the social fund and introduced family credit to ensure that low-income families could no longer be worse off in work than on unemployment benefit. Supplementary benefit was replaced by income support; housing benefit was reformed so that it ceased to discriminate against the low-paid in work and the death grant was abolished and help targeted at low-income groups.

Current Responsibilities
The Department is responsible for the payment of benefits and the collection of contributions under the insurance injuries and national insurance schemes.[13] Family credit and income support are paid on a means-tested basis and the Department is also responsible for the payment of child benefit and one-parent benefit which are not income-related. Other responsibilities include payment of the social fund and a range of non-means-tested contributory benefits and assessing the means of those applying for legal aid.

[13]For further details, see *Social Welfare* (Aspects of Britain: HMSO, 1993).

The Department of Social Security is responsible for making reciprocal social security arrangements with other countries, and for the pensions of British war widows and British war pensioners.

Four executive agencies cover the main aspects of the Department's work: the Benefits Agency, the Contributions Agency, the Child Support Agency, and the Information Technology Services Agency. A fifth agency, the Resettlement Agency, runs residential units designed to help single homeless people and a War Pensions Unit provides services to war pensioners and their widows. The Department's responsibilities cover England, Scotland and Wales but not Northern Ireland.

Non-departmental Public Bodies
The Department sponsors one executive body: the Occupational Pensions Board. Advisory bodies include the War Pensions Committees, the Attendance Allowance Board, the Social Security Advisory Committee, the Disability Living Allowance Advisory Board, the Industrial Injuries Advisory Council, the Pension Law Review Committee and the Pensions Ombudsman. There are seven tribunals: the Vaccine Damage Tribunals, the Disability Appeal Tribunals, the Office of the Social Fund Commissioners, the Office of Social Security Commissioners, the Social Security Appeal Tribunals, the Medical Appeal Tribunals and the Central Adjudication Services.

Offices
The Department of Social Security has been based in Richmond House in Whitehall since 1988. Between 1968 and 1988 it was based at Alexander Fleming House in the Elephant and Castle in south London.

Department of National Heritage

2–4 Cockspur Street, London SW1Y 5DH. Tel: 071–270 3007.

The Department of National Heritage is headed by a Secretary of State, who is a member of the Cabinet. The Secretary of State is currently assisted by a Parliamentary Under-Secretary of State.

Background

The Department was formed in 1992 by absorbing functions from six other departments. It assumed responsibilities for the arts, museums and libraries from the Office of Arts and Libraries, which was dissolved. Sport was acquired from the Department of Education and Science and tourism from the Department of Employment. Responsibility for broadcasting, the press and safety in sports grounds was transferred from the Home Office. Responsibility for the film industry was acquired from the Department of Trade and Industry. Responsibility for royal parks and palaces, historic buildings and ancient monuments was transferred from the Department of the Environment.

The Department published a Green Paper on the future of the BBC (British Broadcasting Corporation) in November 1992. It has also introduced a National Lottery Bill, which would give the Department responsibility for appointing a Director General to regulate the operation of the national lottery.

Current Responsibilities

The Department of National Heritage is responsible for broadcasting, the arts, films and the film industry, press regulation, administration of export licences for antiques and other collectors' items, sport, tourism and heritage.[14] The Department covers issues affecting the arts, including the archaeological and architectural heritage. The funding of museums, galleries and public libraries and the Arts Council fall within its remit, and it is responsible for the construction of a new British Library building at St Pancras.

An executive agency, Historic Royal Palaces, manages those royal palaces that are open to the public. Another executive agency, Royal Parks, is responsible for the royal parks.

The Department has a general responsibility for sport and recreation policy, international sport and sport in England and a specific concern with safety at sports grounds; it also has responsibility for the national lottery and the Millennium Fund.

Responsibility for libraries, tourism, the heritage, museums, galleries and some sports issues (see above) is confined to England. In all other matters the Department's work covers Britain as a whole.

Non-departmental Public Bodies

Executive bodies sponsored by the Department include the Sports Council, the Arts Council, the British Library, the British Museum, the Broadcasting Standards Council, English Heritage, the English Tourist Board, the British Tourist Authority and the Broadcasting Complaints Commission. Advisory bodies include the Library and Information Services Council, the Theatres Trust and the Reviewing Committee on the Export of Works of Art. The

[14]For further information on current broadcasting policies see the forthcoming book *Broadcasting* (Aspects of Britain: HMSO), and for arts policies, see *The Arts* (Aspects of Britain: HMSO, 1993).

Department also sponsors four public corporations: the BBC, the Radio Authority, the Independent Television Commission and S4C (Sianel Pedwar Cymru).

Foreign Affairs and Defence Departments

Foreign and Commonwealth Office

King Charles Street, London SW1 2AH. Tel: 071–270 3000.

The Foreign and Commonwealth Office is headed by the Secretary of State for Foreign and Commonwealth Affairs, who is a member of the Cabinet. At present there is a Minister for Overseas Development, who heads the Overseas Development Administration (see p. 110), three Ministers of State and a Parliamentary Under-Secretary of State.

History and Development

In 1782 the Northern Department, which had been responsible for relations with the Northern Powers of Europe, was reformed as the Foreign Office and made responsible for all foreign issues apart from those relating to the colonies and the Barbary States in North Africa which remained with the Southern Department. The latter department evolved into the Home Department (see p. 75). The department was run by two Under-Secretaries and a chief clerk, supported by a staff of seven clerks. The chief clerk had responsibility for financial matters and was not involved in the department's political work. For many years after 1782 the Foreign Secretary fulfilled his duties with no more than clerical assistance.

He managed the department and dealt with the diplomatic correspondence with a private secretary and a precis writer.

Throughout the eighteenth and nineteenth centuries there were usually two Under-Secretaries. Until 1795 both posts were regarded as political appointments, but after that date one of these posts came to be regarded as permanent and thus did not change hands when a ministry fell. Once this arrangement became accepted the post of Permanent Under-Secretary at the Foreign Office was created. The other Under-Secretaryship developed into a Parliamentary Under-Secretaryship when it became important to have a minister in the House of Commons.

Edmund Hammond (Permanent Under-Secretary 1854–73) established the authority of the Permanent Under-Secretary in the department and his role in providing advice to the Secretary of State on political issues. Under Edmund Hammond most of the department's political work was made answerable to the Permanent Secretary. By 1876 the role of the Parliamentary Under-Secretary became confined to administering parliamentary matters and, sometimes, overseeing the work of the Commercial Department. Hammond also took a major part in establishing rules for admission to the Foreign Office and Diplomatic Service, at the request of the Civil Service Commissioners. In 1856 the Earl of Clarendon (Secretary of State for Foreign Affairs 1853–58, 1865–66 and 1868–70) introduced an entrance examination for junior and supplementary clerks.

In the early twentieth century the Marquess of Lansdowne (Secretary of State for Foreign Affairs 1900–05) relieved senior clerks of the duties of filing and registering papers and gave them a share in the policy-making process, thus ensuring that the talents of able staff were not wasted on clerical and mechanical tasks.

Most commercial functions were transferred to the Department of Overseas Trade, which was created in 1917. However, the Foreign Office retained some responsibility for commerce because this new department was itself jointly responsible to the Foreign Office and the Board of Trade. The arrangement continued until 1946 when the Department of Overseas Trade was dissolved and most of its functions acquired by the Board of Trade.

In 1919 the Diplomatic Service and the Foreign Office were merged to create the Foreign Service. In the same year a separate Commercial Diplomatic Service was also established.

In 1943 Anthony Eden (Secretary of State 1935-38, 1940-45 and 1951-55) continued the trend set by the merger of 1919 by introducing reforms that created a more unified Foreign Service by amalgamating the Commercial Diplomatic Service with the Diplomatic and Consular Services. Eden's reforms broadened the basis of recruitment to the Foreign Office through the provision of pension rights for all employees, family and schooling allowances, and a revised entrance exam. This process was completed in 1946 when the overseas information services of the Ministry of Information were included. As a result of these reforms senior positions in the Foreign Office and abroad were open to staff from all parts of the service.

In the period from the end of the second world war until the late 1960s the administration of Britain's foreign departments experienced many changes as a result of decolonisation and the end of the British Empire. The India Office was abolished in 1947 following the transfer of power to the independent governments of India and Pakistan and its remaining functions were transferred to the Dominions Office to form the Commonwealth Relations Office. In 1966 the Colonial Office, which lost most of its functions as Britain's colonies achieved their independence, merged with the Commonwealth Relations Office to form the Commonwealth Office. In 1968 the Foreign Office and the Commonwealth Office merged to form the Foreign and Commonwealth Office.

In 1961 some of the Foreign Office's responsibilities for economic development were transferred to the Department of Technical Co-operation. In 1964 the Labour Government created the Ministry of Overseas Development from this latter department and gave the new ministry more of the Foreign Office's responsibilities in this field.

The new Conservative Government in 1970 gave overall responsibility for overseas development to the Foreign Office and the Ministry of Overseas Development lost its status as an independent department, although it retained its identity and its own minister within the Foreign and Commonwealth Office. In 1974 the Labour Government re-established a Ministry for Overseas Development; however the new Conservative administration returned overseas development to the Foreign and Commonwealth Office in 1979, reverting to the arrangement of 1970–74.

Policies and Achievements

For much of the nineteenth century British Foreign Secretaries were primarily concerned with the maintenance of a balance of power in Europe and the security of Britain's overseas trade and territories. This was as evident in Lord Castlereagh's support for the Congress System as it was in the efforts of Lords Aberdeen, Palmerston and Salisbury to contain Russian influence in the Near East. But by the 1890s the emergence of France, Russia, and latterly Germany, as imperial rivals, and the division of continental Europe between antagonistic alliances, had seemed in the eyes of

Foreign Office officials to leave Britain dangerously exposed to external pressures. It was to ease the problems of this so-called 'splendid isolation' that Lord Lansdowne concluded an alliance with Japan (1902) and a colonial *entente* with France (1904). His successor, Sir Edward Grey, complemented the Anglo-French agreement with a similar accommodation with Russia (1907), and it was partly in order to ensure the survival of these *ententes* that Britain eventually entered the first world war.

In the wake of the Paris peace settlement (1919–20), British foreign policy was directed towards achieving a reconciliation between former enemies in Europe and rebuilding global peace and stability through the League of Nations. Sir Austen Chamberlain was particularly successful in promoting an Anglo-Franco-German understanding through the Locarno treaties (1925), and his successors continued to pursue the appeasement of Europe. Diplomacy alone could not, however, cope with the menace posed by aggressive and expansive nationalism, and during the 1930s foreign policy was increasingly influenced by military considerations.

Sir Anthony Eden was, as Foreign Secretary in Churchill's wartime coalition, actively engaged both in the creation and maintenance of the grand alliance and in planning for a new world organisation in the shape of the United Nations. But the end of hostilities was followed by the onset of the Cold War, and Ernest Bevin, the new Labour Foreign Secretary (1945–51) was soon involved in a determined effort to retain an American military presence in Europe through what became the NATO alliance. The Foreign Office also had to deal with the numerous issues associated with Britain's global commitments and continuing world role. Meanwhile, the formation of the European Communities and Britain's entry into them have meant that British Foreign

Secretaries have played a leading part in shaping the political and economic structure of modern Europe.

Current Responsibilities

The Foreign and Commonwealth Office is the channel of communication, mainly through the diplomatic service,[15] between the British Government and foreign and Commonwealth[16] governments and international organisations. It is responsible for discussing and negotiating international matters, the protection of British citizens abroad and the defence of British interests overseas. The department monitors overseas developments and assesses their implications, explains British policies to overseas governments and attempts to establish friendly relations with them. It is responsible for funding the BBC World Service. The discharge of Britain's responsibilities to its dependent territories also falls within the department's remit.

Wilton Park (an executive agency) organises international conferences in which professionals from a wide range of backgrounds can engage in off-the-record discussions. In the 1980s the subjects discussed expanded from American and European relations to include Third World problems, North-South relations, East-West relations and developments in the former socialist countries. The agency's Wilton House Conference Centre may be hired by other government departments or private sector organisations.

[15]For further details, see *Overseas Relations and Defence* (Aspects of Britain: HMSO, 1993).
[16] For further details, see *Britain and the Commonwealth* (Aspects of Britain: HMSO, 1992).

Non-departmental Public Bodies

Executive bodies sponsored by the department include the Great Britain–China Centre and the two Commonwealth Institutes. Advisory bodies include the Diplomatic Service Appeals Board and the Government Hospitality Fund Advisory Committee for the Purchase of Wine. Tribunals include the Foreign Compensation Commission. Other non-departmental public bodies are sponsored by the Overseas Development Administration (see p. 110).

Offices

In 1782 the Foreign Office was accommodated in two houses in Cleveland Row, St James's, which had been occupied by the Northern and Southern Secretaries of State. Increases in the volume of its work necessitated a move to the Cockpit, Whitehall, in 1786 and a further shift to offices in Downing Street where the department moved into Lord Sheffield's former home.

The Foreign Office acquired more houses in Downing Street and expanded into Fludyer Street in 1793. Unfortunately the foundations of these houses were weak and large cracks appeared in the walls and ceilings. One house collapsed and the others had to be supported by wooden posts. In 1839 the buildings of the Foreign Office and the Colonial Office, which was also located in Downing Street, were condemned as unfit and unsafe by a report from the Select Committee on Public Offices.

In 1858, following a government competition launched two years earlier, Gilbert Scott was appointed as architect of a new Foreign Office building to be built on the Downing Street site. Scott favoured a Gothic-style building but was overruled by Palmerston who insisted on a building in the classical style.

Construction began in 1861–62 and the Foreign Office moved to temporary accommodation in Whitehall Gardens. The new building was opened in 1868 and the Foreign Office moved into its new home next to the India Office, which had been built the previous year. In 1875 the office block was extended to Whitehall with the construction of new Colonial Office and Home Office buildings.

In the 1920s a shortage of accommodation led to the construction of a new storey; however this was only a temporary solution to the shortage of space which grew steadily worse. In 1947 the Foreign Office acquired more accommodation when it obtained the India Office for its German Department following the abolition of that ministry. The Government proposed to demolish Scott's building in 1963 but was prevented and it was eventually classified as a Grade 1 listed building.

Following the merger with the Commonwealth Office in 1968 and the departure of the Home Office for Queen Anne's Gate in 1978, the Foreign and Commonwealth Office occupied all of the accommodation that had once housed the Foreign Office, the India Office, the Home Office and the Colonial Office. A programme of refurbishment and restoration is in progress and is scheduled for completion in about 1995.

Ministry of Defence

Main Building, Whitehall, London SW1A 2HB. Tel 071–218 9000.

The Ministry is headed by a Secretary of State, who is a Cabinet minister. The Secretary of State is currently assisted by Ministers of State for the Armed Forces and for Procurement and by a Parliamentary Under-Secretary of State.

History and Development

The Ministry of Defence (MOD) is a relatively new creation. Until 1964 there were five Departments of State doing what the unified MOD does today: the Ministry of Defence, the Admiralty, the War Office, the Air Ministry and the Ministry of Aviation. In 1964 the first four were amalgamated, and the defence functions of the Ministry of Aviation Supply (as it had by then become) were taken over in 1971, when the MOD took over responsibility for supplying military aircraft and guided weapons.

The oldest of these departments was the Admiralty, responsible for the Navy. In 1546 Henry VIII created a Navy Board to oversee the administrative affairs of the naval service; other matters remained in the hands of the Lord High Admiral. From 1628 this post was usually filled by a 'committee' of Lords Commissioners—the Board of Admiralty. Its head was the First Lord, the Minister who was the political master of the Navy. For more than two centuries the Navy was run by these two Boards, under a system devised largely by Samuel Pepys.

Relations between the two Boards were not always harmonious. In 1832 the Navy Board was abolished and its functions brought under the superintendence of the Board of Admiralty. In the eighteenth century the department moved to the building in Whitehall still called the Old Admiralty.

The War Office, responsible for the Army, was originally the 'Secretary at War's Office'. The first holder of the post was killed in battle—at sea—against the Dutch in 1666. It became of increasing importance in the political control of the Army, although it was not the only government department involved.

Finally in 1854 the War Office was set up to take over all political and financial control of the Army. After many years of gradual change the War Office was finally reformed in 1904 on the lines of the Board of Admiralty, with the Secretary of State chairing the Army Council.

The Air Ministry was created in January 1918 to oversee the birth in April 1918 of the Royal Air Force from the amalgamation of the Royal Flying Corps and the Royal Naval Air Service. The organisation was broadly similar to that of the Admiralty and the War Office with a Secretary of State chairing the Air Council and the senior RAF member holding the post of Chief of Staff.

The supply of military aircraft, which had been the responsibility of the Air Ministry, was transferred in 1940 to a new Ministry of Aircraft Production, which in 1946 was amalgamated with the Ministry of Supply. In further reorganisations the task was switched to the Ministry of Aviation in 1959, to the Ministry of Technology in 1967 and finally to the Ministry of Aviation Supply in 1970. In 1971 the Government called on Derek Rayner to advise on its relations with the aviation industry. One of his principal recommendations was the transfer to the MOD of the military aviation task, to be undertaken by a separate organisation within the MOD, which would also assume the responsibility for all other military procurement. The resulting Procurement Executive was formed in 1971. In 1985 a unified defence staff was established which assumed many of the functions of the single Service staffs.

Policies and Achievements

Britain's defence policy is a key component of its wider security policy.[17] Its purpose remains to contribute to maintaining the freedom and territorial integrity of Britain and its dependent territories, and its ability to pursue its legitimate interests and activities at home and abroad.

Britain's independent nuclear deterrent provides the ultimate guarantee of its security. The Vanguard Class Trident missile submarine is replacing the ageing Polaris fleet, and will provide its deterrent needs, at the minimum level, well into the next century.

Since 1946 the Ministry of Defence has organised British involvement in several military operations, recent examples being the Falklands campaign in 1982 and the participation of British forces in the liberation of Kuwait in 1991.

Current Responsibilities

The Ministry of Defence is responsible for the control, administration, equipment and support of Britain's armed forces. The Ministry's Procurement Executive handles the research, development, production and purchase of equipment and weapons for the armed forces.

The Defence Analytical Services Agency (an executive agency) provides, through its manpower section, current and historic manpower statistics to help in monitoring the Ministry's budget, developing personnel policy and deciding manpower resourcing issues.

The Royal Navy is supplied with hydrographic and oceanographic information by the Hydrographic Office, a defence support

[17]For further details, see *Overseas Relations and Defence* (Aspects of Britain: HMSO, 1993).

agency. This office also supplies publications and charts to the Merchant Navy and other non-naval bodies. Other executive and defence support agencies include the Army Base Repair Organisation, the Meteorological Office, the Duke of York's Royal Military School, the Defence Research Agency, RAF Maintenance, the Directorate General of Defence Accounts, the Defence Operational Analysis Centre, the Naval Aircraft Repair Organisation, the Military Survey, Queen Victoria School, the Defence Postal and Courier Service and the Chemical and Biological Defence Establishment, which is Britain's scientific and technical authority on chemical and biological defence issues.

Another executive agency, the Service Children's Schools (North West Europe), is responsible for the educational requirements of children of service personnel and some civilians based in that region.

Non-departmental Public Bodies

Executive bodies sponsored by the department include the National Army Museum, the Royal Naval Museum and the Royal Air Force Museum.

Offices

The headquarters of the Ministry of Defence were housed in Great George Street from its creation in 1946 to 1948 when it moved to Storey's Gate. In 1964 the headquarters of the ministry were moved into its present accommodation in the Main Building in Whitehall.

Overseas Development Administration

94 Victoria Street, London SW1E 5JL. Tel: 071–917 7000.

The department is run by the Minister for Overseas Development, who is also a Minister of State at the Foreign and Commonwealth Office.

History and Development

The present Overseas Development Administration (ODA) came into being in 1979 when the Secretary of State for Foreign and Commonwealth Affairs assumed full responsibility for the overseas development work previously carried out by the Ministry of Overseas Development (ODM) and the ODA became a functional wing of the Foreign and Commonwealth Office.

Policies and Achievements

Since 1989 Baroness Chalker of Wallasey has been Minister for Overseas Development. During this period, increasing emphasis has been placed on the concept of 'good government' in developing countries. These include respect for human rights and the rule of law, administrative competence and accountability. Lady Chalker has linked the giving of aid to a country's record on human rights and democratic institutions.

The other priorities which underlie the aid programme are the principles of helping the poorest, and support for sustainable economic and social development through economic reform in developing countries; assistance to health and population programmes and for the role of women in development; and the protection and preservation of the natural environment for future generations.

Barbara Castle (Minister for Overseas Development 1964–65) introduced loans to developing countries on terms more favourable than those given by almost any other industrialised country. All Britain's new aid to the poorest countries is now given in the form of grants rather than loans.

Current Responsibilities

The ODA is responsible for managing Britain's aid programme to developing countries. Britain spends over £1,800 million a year on development aid in partnership with over 130 developing countries. This assistance is given through projects—to increase agricultural production or develop power and water supplies, for example; through finance to supply essential materials and equipment; and in the form of technical co-operation to develop human skills and improve local institutions by providing expert advice or special training. Aid is either provided directly or channelled through international organisations such as the European Community and the United Nations and its specialist agencies. Assistance is also channelled through non-governmental organisations, known as NGOs. The department is also responsible for emergency aid to countries suffering the effects of natural and man-made disasters and for the payment of overseas pensions. The ODA is also responsible for the Global Environmental Programme which helps developing countries contribute to global environmental improvements.

The ODA's executive agency, the Natural Resources Institute, based at Chatham, carries out research and practical scientific work to help developing countries achieve sustainable management of their renewable natural resources. Although most of its work is carried out on behalf of the ODA, it also works on a contract basis for international agencies and other organisations.

Territorial Departments

The Northern Ireland Office

Stormont, Belfast BT4 3TT. Tel: 0232 763255.
Whitehall, London SW1A 2AZ. Tel: 071–210 3000.

The Northern Ireland Office is run by a Secretary of State, who is a member of the Cabinet. At present there are also two Ministers of State and two Parliamentary Under-Secretaries of State.[18]

History and Development

The British Government attempted to establish legislative and administrative devolution for all of Ireland through the three Home Rule Bills of 1886, 1893 and 1912. The third Bill was passed by Parliament in 1914 but was not implemented due to the outbreak of war in Europe. After the war the south of Ireland achieved full independence from Britain and Northern Ireland was granted a system of devolved legislation and administration.

In 1920 the Government of Ireland Act delegated many legislative and executive powers to a Northern Ireland Government based at Stormont. The services transferred were assigned to Northern Ireland Departments by formal notification of the Lord Lieutenant in 1921 and local ministries were established for agriculture, education, commerce, labour and national insurance,

[18]For further details see *Northern Ireland* (Aspects of Britain: HMSO, 1992).

health and local government, finance and home affairs. Westminster retained control over foreign and defence matters, issues affecting the Crown and some other matters such as coinage and the Post Office. These constitutional arrangements survived for over 50 years until persistent inter-communal violence led the British Government to assume responsibility for law and order in 1972. The Northern Ireland Government resigned in protest against this decision and the British Government imposed direct rule.

The Northern Ireland Office, which took over all the functions vested in the Northern Ireland Government and Parliament, had a wide brief which covered finance, commerce, agriculture, health, social security, education, development, community relations, home affairs and security policy.

Policies and Achievements

Attempts have been made by successive British governments to find a means of restoring a widely acceptable form of devolved government to Northern Ireland. In 1973 William Whitelaw (Secretary of State 1972–74) established a power-sharing executive under Brian Faulkner; however this collapsed in May 1974 and there has been no devolution since.

Merlyn Rees (Secretary of State 1974–76) set up a Constitutional Convention, but it failed to agree on a system of government that would command widespread support. In 1980 a political conference established by Humphrey Atkins (1979–81) also failed to reach agreement. In 1982 a Northern Ireland Assembly was created by James Prior (1981–84) and given responsibility for making proposals for devolving powers on a basis which would command widespread acceptance throughout the community. However, the Unionist parties, who had a large majority in the Assembly, decided not to fulfil the Assembly's statutory duties in 1986 as a protest against the Anglo-Irish Agreement (see below) and the British Government dissolved it later the same year.

In 1985 Britain and the Irish Republic signed the Anglo-Irish Agreement, which affirmed that no change in the status of Northern Ireland would come about except by the consent of a majority of its people. The Agreement also established an Intergovernmental Conference, through which the Irish Government could put forward views and proposals on specified matters affecting Northern Ireland affairs.

The Conference has met frequently and discusses a wide range of issues affecting Northern Ireland affairs. It also acts as a forum for promoting cross-border co-operation, especially on security.

Peter Brooke (Secretary of State 1989–92) and Sir Patrick Mayhew (Secretary of State since 1992) have held a series of talks with the main constitutional parties in Northern Ireland and the Irish Government with the aim of securing a comprehensive political settlement that would take account of relationships within Northern Ireland, within the island of Ireland and between the two Governments. Consultations are continuing in order to take the process forward during 1993.

The Northern Ireland Office has played a key role in attracting industry to the province and developing the region's economy. In this task the department has been assisted by the Northern Ireland Development Agency and its successor and the Northern Ireland Industrial Development Board, both of which it sponsored.

Under Labour Secretaries of State Merlyn Rees (1974–76) and Roy Mason (1976–79) the Northern Ireland Office introduced fair employment legislation to end religious discrimination by employers. During Roy Mason's tenure at the Northern Ireland Office the laws on divorce and homosexuality were brought into line with those in the rest of Britain and the courts system was reformed.

Current Responsibilities

The Secretary of State for Northern Ireland has direct responsibility through the Northern Ireland Office for constitutional developments, law and order, security and electoral matters.

Under the 1974 Northern Ireland Act the six Northern Ireland departments, which were established by the 1920 Act, are also subject to the direction and control of the Secretary of State while direct rule continues. The Northern Ireland departments, all of which are based in Northern Ireland, are listed below.

Department of Agriculture for Northern Ireland

This department is responsible for agricultural policy and agricultural development, the forestry and fishing industries, rural development and the veterinary, scientific and advisory services. It also administers European Community support and other arrangements including education and training.

Department for Economic Development for Northern Ireland

The Department is responsible for developing industry and commerce in the province. It also administers government policy on tourism, energy, minerals, industrial relations and research and technology, employment equality, consumer protection, health and safety at work and company legislation. An employment service and training schemes are administered through the Training and

Employment Agency (an executive agency). The Industrial Development Board for Northern Ireland administers assistance to industry for this department.

Department of Education for Northern Ireland

The Department has responsibility for education from nursery to higher and continuing education as well as control over the five education and library boards. It also covers youth services, sport and recreation, cultural activities and the development of community relations within and between schools.

Department of the Environment for Northern Ireland

The Department is concerned with environmental protection, housing, planning, the construction and maintenance of roads, transport, traffic management and vehicle licensing and taxation, including the Driver and Vehicle Testing Agency, which is an executive agency. It is also responsible for harbours, water and sewerage functions, the maintenance of public records, certain controls over local government, and the Ordnance Survey of Northern Ireland and the Rate Collection Agency (both executive agencies).

Department of Finance and Personnel

The Department of Finance and Personnel is responsible for the control of the province's public expenditure, economic and social research and analysis, charities, the Valuation and Lands Offices (an executive agency), equal opportunities, personnel management policies and the general management and control of the Northern Ireland Civil Service. This department liaises with the Treasury and the Northern Ireland Office over financial matters and is responsible for the co-ordination of European Community policies.

Department of Health and Social Services for Northern Ireland
The Department is responsible for policy on health, personal social services, social legislation and the Office of the Registrar General. The Management Executive is responsible for the implementation of policy through the health and social services boards. The Social Security Agency, an executive agency, is responsible for the administration and payment of all social security benefits and the collection of National Insurance contributions. Another executive agency, the Child Support Agency, is responsible for the assessment, collection and enforcement of maintenance to children.

Non-departmental Public Bodies

Executive bodies sponsored by the department include the Police Authority for Northern Ireland, the Labour Relations Agency, the Agricultural Wages Board for Northern Ireland, the Northern Ireland Tourist Board, the Equal Opportunities Commission for Northern Ireland and the Northern Ireland Housing Executive.

Advisory bodies include the Northern Ireland Boundary Commission, the Northern Ireland Water Council, the Historic Monuments Council and the Local Government Staff Commission. Tribunals include the Rent Assessment Panel, the Water Appeals Commission and the Planning Appeals Commission.

Offices

The Northern Ireland Office is based in the Stormont complex which once housed the Northern Ireland Government and Parliament. In London the Northern Ireland Office was first situated in Great George Street and in 1984 moved to Whitehall.

The Scottish Office

St Andrew's House, Edinburgh EH1 3DG. Tel: 031–556 8400.
Dover House, Whitehall, London SW1A 2AU. Tel: 071–270 3000.

The Scottish Office is run by a Secretary of State, who is a member of the Cabinet. The department currently has a Minister of State and three Parliamentary Under-Secretaries of State.

The distinctive character of Scotland and the fact that it has a separate legal system means that separate Scottish legislation is enacted on many issues. Special Scottish provisions are also inserted in Acts of Parliament applying to the whole of Britain.

History and Development

After the enactment of the 1707 Treaty of Union, which abolished the independent Scottish Parliament, the British Government created the post of Secretary of State for Scottish Affairs. Following the Jacobite rising in 1745 this post was abolished and nominal ministerial responsibility for Scottish matters was transferred to British ministries, although the influence of the Scottish political figures like the Lord Advocate and the Scottish Manager was still important. In 1827 control of Scottish matters passed to the Home Office where it remained for nearly 60 years.

Nevertheless, Scotland retained control of some administrative functions and the Lord Advocate remained head of the Scottish system of public prosecution and enjoyed some political responsibilities which were ill-defined and whose scope depended on the prestige and character of the individual Lord Advocate (see p. 72). Scottish boards were created to deal with issues like prisons, the poor law, fisheries, education and lunacy.

During the nineteenth century Scottish discontent with the way Scotland was governed increased and demands were made for the appointment of a Scottish Secretary with powers similar to those of the Irish Secretary. In 1885 the Secretary of Scotland Act established a Scottish Office and a Scottish Secretary. The Act did not define the minister's powers and duties but instead transferred the Scottish functions of the Home Office, the Privy Council, the Treasury and the Local Government Board to the new Scottish Office. In 1892 the Scottish Secretary was made a member of the Cabinet. In 1926 the post of Scottish Secretary was upgraded to Secretary of State for Scotland.

By 1914 there was concern that the Scottish Office did not have enough control over the large number of Scottish boards. The Commission on the Civil Service proposed that the boards should be abolished and replaced with civil servants reporting direct to ministers. In 1928 these proposals were put into effect. The new Scottish Departments of Health and Agriculture and the Prisons Department were to act under the direction and control of the Secretary of State but were to retain their own statutory existence. This system was, however, short-lived and in 1939 the Departments lost their independence and were incorporated within a new Scottish Office.

The 1939 Act created a flexible structure which allowed the Secretary of State to change departments or shift functions between the four departments which covered agriculture, education, health and home affairs. In 1962 the functions of the Home and Health Departments were redistributed into a Home and Health Department and a Development Department. In 1974 the Scottish Office was reorganised into five departments and an Economic Planning Department was created. In 1984 the

Economic Planning Department became the Industry Department and in 1991 the Development Department was replaced by the Environment Department.

Policies and Achievements

The Scottish Office has played a key role in developing the poorer areas of the country. For example, Thomas Johnson (Secretary of State 1941–45) created the North of Scotland Hydro-Electric Board (1943) and William Ross (1964–70 and 1974–76) established the Highlands and Islands Development Board in 1965 and the Scottish Development Agency in 1976.

Bruce Millan (1976–79) introduced devolution legislation that would have established a Scottish Assembly with a wide range of social and environmental powers, including health, the social services (but not social security benefits), transport (but not the railways), housing, planning, roads and various Home Office responsibilities. Although 51.6 per cent of those voting supported devolution in a referendum in March 1979 this did not meet the level required by legislation of 40 per cent of the electorate and the Assembly plan was not implemented.

Current Responsibilities

The Scottish Office's responsibilities are discharged mainly through its five departments, all based in Edinburgh.[19]

Department of Agriculture and Fisheries

This department covers the promotion of the agricultural and fishing industries. It contains two executive agencies: the Scottish

[19]For further information, see *Scotland* (Aspects of Britain: HMSO, 1993).

Agricultural Scientific Services Agency; and the Scottish Fisheries Protection Agency, which is responsible for the enforcement of fisheries laws and regulations.

Environment Department

The Environment Department has responsibility for environmental protection, nature conservation, the countryside, land-use planning, water supplies, sewerage, local government including finance, housing, building control and the presentation to the public and protection of historic buildings and ancient monuments through Historic Scotland, which is an executive agency.

Home and Health Department

The Home and Health Department is concerned with the central administration of law and order (including the police service), criminal justice, legal aid and penal institutions through the Scottish Prison Service, an executive agency. The NHS, the fire service, home defence, the civil emergency services and social work services also fall within the Department's remit. The Scottish Office Pensions Agency is responsible for pensions for, among others, teachers and NHS employees.

Education Department

The Education Department is responsible for all educational institutions apart from the universities. Student grants, the arts, libraries, museums, galleries, the Gaelic language and sport and recreation are also within its brief.

Industry Department

The Industry Department covers industrial and regional economic development, employment, training, energy, tourism, urban regeneration, new towns, roads and certain transport functions (particularly in the Highlands and Islands) and the co-ordination of Scottish Office European interests.

Central Services Division

A Central Services division includes the Office of the Solicitor to the Secretary of State and the Scottish Office Information Directorate. Administrative Services, the Personnel Group and the Finance Group are also included in Central Services.

Other Departments

There are also four small departments for which the Secretary of State has a degree of responsibility. The Scottish Record Office, an executive agency, is responsible for a range of administrative, legal and other records. The Scottish Courts Administration has responsibility for the organisation, administration and staffing of the Supreme Court and the Sheriff courts and court offices. This latter department is also responsible to the Lord Advocate for some functions (see p. 72). The General Register Office for Scotland is the Scottish equivalent of the Office of Population Censuses and Surveys. The Department of the Registers of Scotland (an executive agency) is responsible for compiling public registers of legal documents.

The Secretary of State is responsible for the activities in Scotland of several government bodies, such as the Forestry Commission, whose remit extends beyond Scotland.

Non-departmental Public Bodies

Executive bodies sponsored by the Scottish Office include Highlands and Islands Enterprise, Scottish Enterprise, the Scottish Tourist Board, the Crofters Commission, the Scottish Legal Aid Board and the Countryside Commission for Scotland. Advisory bodies include the Advisory Committee on Scotland's Travelling People and the Consultative Committee on Freshwater Fisheries for Scotland. There are five tribunals: the Children's Panels, the Horse Race Betting Levy Appeal Tribunal for Scotland, the Rent Assessment Panel for Scotland, the National Health Service Tribunal for Scotland and the National Appeal Panel for Entry to Pharmaceutical Lists for Scotland.

Offices

Following the passage of the Reorganisation of Offices (Scotland) Act in 1939 St Andrew's House was opened as the Scottish Office's headquarters in Scotland. In 1975 the department's headquarters were moved to new offices at New St Andrew's House, although some functions continued to be run from St Andrew's House. In 1988 the ministerial offices were returned to St Andrew's House. A few liaison staff are based in Dover House, which was the original office of the Secretary of State in 1885 and remains the base for ministers while Parliament is sitting.

The Welsh Office

Cathays Park, Cardiff CF1 3NQ. Tel: 0222 825111.
Gwydyr House, Whitehall, London SW1A 2ER. Tel: 071–270 3000.

The Welsh Office is headed by a Secretary of State, who is a member of the Cabinet. At present the Secretary of State is assisted by a Minister of State and a Parliamentary Under-Secretary of State.

History and Development

The origins of the Welsh Office lie in the creation of 'Welsh sections in other departments. The first of these was the 'Welsh Department' in the Board of Education which was formed in 1907. In 1919 a 'Welsh Department' in the Ministry of Agriculture and a Welsh Board of Health were added.

Wartime conditions led to increased devolution and by 1945 a further 15 departments had established offices in Wales. After the second world war the emphasis was placed on improving departmental liaison between the Welsh departments, and an enlarged role was given to Welsh advisory bodies. In 1948 the Labour Government created the Council for Wales and Monmouthshire. This body was composed of representatives from the local authorities, industry and other interests. However, progress towards a unified Welsh Office was slow. In 1951 the Conservative Government recognised the growing importance of Welsh matters by adding Welsh affairs to the portfolio of the Home Secretary (Sir David Maxwell Fyfe). In 1957 the Conservative Government transferred responsibility for Welsh affairs to the Minister of Housing and Local Government and appointed a Minister of State for Welsh Affairs. But these reforms did not satisfy a growing number of people who thought that Wales should be given its own department. In the same year (1957) the Council for Wales and Monmouthshire endorsed the campaign for a Welsh Office. They argued that there was too little co-ordination of the activities of the Welsh departments and that only the creation of a Welsh Office could solve these problems.

In its 1959 general election manifesto the Labour Party included a pledge to create a Welsh Office; although it lost the election Labour retained its commitment to this proposal and implemented the plan shortly after winning the 1964 General Election. The first Secretary of State for Wales was Jim Griffiths who had been a long-standing advocate of a Welsh Office.

Opponents of a powerful Welsh Office argued that the Secretary of State for Wales should do no more than oversee the activities of 'Welsh Departments' in other ministries. The Labour Government rejected this notion of a Welsh Office confined to an oversight role and announced in 1964 that a Welsh Office was to be formed from the regional branch of the Ministry of Housing and Local Government together with the Welsh roads division of the Ministry of Transport.

In 1968 the Welsh Office acquired responsibility for some agricultural matters. In 1969 health and welfare responsibilities were added; they were followed in 1970 by primary and secondary education and child care in 1971. Substantial industrial functions were acquired in 1975 and responsibilities for higher education and manpower were added in 1978. In the same year the department obtained full responsibility for agriculture and fisheries.

Policies and Achievements

In the late 1970s the Welsh Office sponsored legislation which if implemented would have surrendered some of the department's powers to a new Welsh Assembly. Under the proposals the Assembly would have acquired a range of social and environmental functions similar to those devolved to its Scottish counterpart.

However, the Welsh Assembly was not to be granted full legislative control in these areas and the Secretary of State for Wales was to retain a great deal of control. This limited form of devolution was not brought into effect because the proposal was defeated in a referendum in March 1979.

Since its creation the Welsh Office has played a role in developing the Welsh economy. Under the 1974–79 Labour Government the department established the Welsh Development Agency, which was charged with attracting industry to Wales. Between 1987 and 1990 Peter Walker, a Conservative Secretary of State, launched a series of initiatives to promote Wales and attract industry to the Principality. His Valleys Initiative encompassed a wide range of schemes from derelict land clearance and road construction to the building of new schools and hospitals.

Current Responsibilities

The department has responsibility for a wide range of Welsh affairs.[20] These include health, community care and personal social services and all educational matters apart from the terms and conditions of service, student awards and the University of Wales. The Welsh language and cultural issues also fall within its remit along with agriculture and fisheries, forestry, local government, housing, sport, water and sewerage.

Other responsibilities include environmental subjects: environmental protection, the countryside, nature conservation and land use (including town and country planning) are all part of its brief. The department's responsibilities over monuments and historic buildings are exercised through CADW (Welsh Historic

[20]For further information, see *Wales* (Aspects of Britain: HMSO, 1993).

Monuments), which is an executive agency. The Welsh Planning Inspectorate is also organised as an executive agency and handles public inquiries and appeals on planning, housing, environmental protection, highways and other Welsh matters.

The Welsh Office is responsible for a range of economic functions. This covers selective financial assistance to industry, the urban programme, urban investment grants in Wales, regional planning in Wales, the oversight of economic affairs and the operation of the European Regional Development Fund in Wales and other European Community matters. Enterprise and training are also included along with tourism, roads, women's issues in Wales and civil emergencies. In addition, the department is responsible for all financial aspects of these matters including the Welsh revenue support grant.

Non-departmental Public Bodies

Executive bodies sponsored by the department include the National Library of Wales, the National Museum of Wales, the Royal Commission on Ancient and Historical Monuments in Wales, the Wales Tourist Board, the Cardiff Bay Development Corporation, the Welsh Development Agency, the Welsh Sports Council and the Curriculum Council for Wales.

Advisory bodies include the Welsh Language Board, the Ancient Monuments Board for Wales, the Welsh Dental Committee, the Welsh Committee on Drug Misuse, the Urban Investment Grant Appraisal Panel, the Wales Committee for Postgraduate Pharmaceutical Education and the Training, Enterprise and the Education Advisory Group for Wales.

There are four tribunals: the Agricultural Land Tribunal (Wales), the Valuation and Community Charge Tribunal (Wales), the Mental Health Review Tribunal for Wales and the Rent Assessment Panel.

Offices
In 1964 the Welsh Office was established at 47 Parliament Street in London and at Cathays Park in Cardiff. In 1971 the London office moved to Gwydyr House in Whitehall.

Further Reading

£

Britain and the European Community.
George, Stephen.
ISBN 0 19 827315 0.   Clarendon Press Oxford   1992   30.00

British Government: The Central Executive Territory.
Madgwick, Peter.
ISBN 0 86003 716.   Philip Allen   1991   9.95

British Policy in Northern Ireland 1968–89.
Cunningham, Michael.
ISBN 0 7190 2568 0.   Manchester University Press   1991   40.00

The Case for the Crown.
Rozenberg, Joshua.
ISBN 85336 0112.   Equation   1987   12.95

The Future of Whitehall.
MacDonald, Oonagh.
ISBN 0 297 81240 8.   Weidenfeld and Nicholson   1992   19.99

Inside the Foreign Office.
Dickie, John.
ISBN 1 85592 550 8.   Chapmans   1992   20.00

Inside the Think Tank.
Blackstone, Tessa and Plowden, William.
ISBN 0 434 07490 X.   William Heinemann   1988   14.95

£

The Lord Chancellor.
ISBN 0 900963 81 6.   Terence Dalton   1978   99p

(Part of the *Offices of State* series, which also includes titles on the Chancellor of the Exchequer, the Secretary of State, the Admiralty and the Foreign Secretary.)

Whitehall.
Hennessy, Peter.
ISBN 0 436 19271 3.   Secker and Warburg   1989   20.00

The *New Whitehall Series*, which consists of authoritative descriptions of the major departments and was published in the 1960s and 1970s by George Allen and Unwin Ltd, contains valuable historical information.

Annuals
Public Bodies   Cabinet Office
Civil Service Year Book   HMSO

Printed in the UK for HMSO.
Dd.0296536, 7/93, C3, 51-2423, 5673.